small faces

the young mods' forgotten story

".....beautifully presented and impeccably researched...
placing them alongside the BEATLES, STONES, WHO
ET AL as one of the 60's absolute staples." **N.M.E.**

"Stocked with anecdotes and a clear perspective,
this book serves the Small Faces' memory well." **SELECT**

**ACID
JAZZ**

Having penned numerous words of wit and wisdom for both the *NME* and *Melody Maker*, written a bestselling biography of The Jam entitled *A Beat Concerto* and a novel entitled *Heaven's Promise*, Paolo Hewitt was enticed out of retirement after *The South Bank Show* threatened to run a programme on his collected works. A staunch defender of Spurs, Napoli, Woking FC, hip-hop, Brutus shirts and his friends, Paolo is the proud father of Sarah Jane Bacchuss and aims one day to buy 22 Westmoreland Terrace, Pimlico. He is currently working on a new novel whilst plotting the best way with which to bring down the British class system. He is single, lives in London and still has big blue eyes.

small faces

Paolo Hewitt

WITH A FOREWORD BY KENNEY JONES

ACID JAZZ

acknowledgements

This book could not have been written without the invaluable help and assistance of Kenney Jones, Ian Mclagan and Ronnie Lane who not only made the records but found the time to talk about them and the lives they once led. Many thanks.

The same applies to the following numbers:

Terry Rawlings for his inspired picture research, numerous contacts and access to unpublished interviews.

Paul 'Bullseye' Weller for access to his batcave, top support and making that tape so many years ago.

Johnny Chandler for suggestions, encouragement and solid behaviour when it came to his memorabilia.

Gavin Dodds and *Beverley Cousins* for their Mod like attention to detail in designing and editing this book so brilliantly.

Bob Morris for his determination to see this book on the shelves after all the delays - for not letting it go "up the pictures"!

Thumbs up also to:

Andrew Arnhem Ogden's Newsletter, 5 Hogshill Lane, Cobham, Surrey, KT11 2AG

Andy Neill for cool and helpful research, his brother *Chris* for the down under stories and *Alan* and *Katherine Wright* for the photos.

Photos and memorabilia from the private collections of:

Kenney Jones, Paul Weller, Terry Rawlings, Steve Chamberlain, Marco Nelson, Dave Lawson, Johnny Chandler, Andrew Arnhem, Alan and Katherine Wright, Melody Maker and N.M.E.

Personal thanks to:

Eddie Piller, Anne Marie Bigby, Bunyard for his shopping expeditions, Mark Lusty, Bobby G., Noel Gallagher, Jeff Barrett, Tony Gale, Pat Gilbert at Record Collector, Paul Hallam, Damon Albarn and Andy Bell. John Hellier, Julie & Charmaine at Funky Feet, MRM Graphics, Stuart & Jo at Airlift & everyone at Acid Jazz Records.

This book is dedicated to the timeless music of Steve Marriott and Ronnie Lane

First published in the U.K. by Acid Jazz Books
1st edition July 1995
Reprinted November 1995
a division of Re-Elect The President Limited
1 Hoxton Square, Hoxton, London, N1 6NV

ISBN 0 9523935 0 6

Edited by Beverley Cousins
Book designed by Gavin Dodds
Jacket designed by Terry Rawlings
Printed by Commercial Colour Press
116-118 Woodgrange Road
Forest Gate, London E7 0EW
Production Controller Bob Morris

Distributed by Airlift Book Company
26-28 Eden Grove, London N7 8EF

Picture acknowledgements

Gered Mankowitz
Pages: 17, 43, 97, 103, 105, 117, 120, 121, 122, 124, 133, 137

Tony Gale, Pictorial Press, 13 Berners Street, London, W1P 3DE
Front & Back Cover and Pages: 10, 12, 41, 48, 51, 57, 61, 64 (top and bottom), 65, 67, 69, 72, 74, 77, 98, 101, 150, 152, 158 Colour section one, pages: 2 (top and bottom), 5, 6, 7, 8, 9, 11, 12, 13, 15 (top and bottom) Colour section two, pages: 1, 4, 7, 9, 10, 12, 13 (top), 15 (bottom)

Chris Clunn, Working Out Of Joy, Unit 17, Aberdeen Studios, 22 Highbury Grove, London, N5
Page 2

Every effort has been made by the publishers to credit organisations and individuals with regard to the supply of photographs and illustrations. The publishers apologise for any omissions arising from their inability to trace the original photographers and artists.

contents

Well it's about time that someone wrote a book on The Small Faces. Finally, we have been recognised as one of the great bands of the sixties, and who knows, maybe one day someone will give us a Grammy or an Ivor Novello! It's ironic that we have all received various awards for other bands we have been in but none ever came The Small Faces' way. (Surely we're due a lifetime achievement award before we're too old to receive it!) The Small Faces were pioneers who paved the way for so many other bands. Unfortunately, we paid the price. Looking back we were certainly ahead of our time. Many years have now passed but The Small Faces material still holds up to this day. I'm glad that we have finally been documented in this book and that our story has at last been told, but I have to say that words cannot describe the emotional fulfillment I had as a founder member of the group. I still miss Steve, Ronnie and Mac.

Now are you ready? Good, then we'll begin.

Kenney Jones, May 1994.

This book is dedicated to the timeless music of
Steve Marriott and Ronnie Lane.

One of the first pictures of Steve Marriott and Ronnie Lane
together, only a few weeks after they met.
Taken outside Ronnie's parents' home, July 1965.

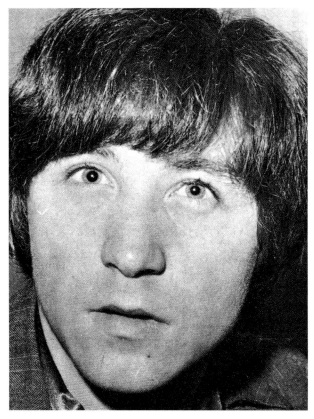

Kenney Jones.

Thursday afternoon, July 1993, a wine bar in London's Holborn area.

Kenney Jones, drummer, enters with Terry Rawlings. This is the first time that Terry, a key researcher for this book, has arranged for Jones and me to meet.

Contrary to the drummer stereotype, Jones is a soft-spoken, likeable and, as befits a member of The Small Faces, diminutive man. He now lives in Surrey, a far cry from the tough Locksley Estate in Stepney, east London, where he was raised. His mum, incidentally, still resides there, staunchly refusing to move out.

These days Jones, who maintains various business interests, has become the official custodian of The Small Faces. He spends much of his time trying to sort out the financial and contractual mess that the group left behind when they disbanded in 1969. Not because he needs the money, but because the other surviving members might. Twenty-six years on and the spirit of friendship that bound the group together still exerts a great hold on him.

When The Small Faces fell apart, Jones went on to play with two of pop music's most memorable groups, The Faces and The Who. It is from the latter that he finally earned the kind of money it's assumed all musicians make. Now, after a period of isolation, he is keen to resume his musical career. In a couple of months' time, he will play on a session with Primal Scream. The following year, just weeks after appearing on stage with Paul Weller and the group Mother Earth, for a rousing rendition of one of The Small Faces' greatest songs, 'Rollin' Over', he will fly out to America to discuss a proposed Faces reformation.

Today he is here to look over the manuscript so far, clear up any errors and add more information if needed. He orders a beer and I hand over the work to date.

As he peruses the copy, I decide to throw him various questions pertaining to The Small Faces. He's already told me that his next appointment is not for at least another hour and I want to make the most of his available time.

After fielding a few enquiries, Jones finishes his beer. I ask him if he wants another. He declines. Instead, he asks where the toilets are. When he returns it is obvious from his expression that something is troubling him.

'I'm sorry,' he announces unexpectedly, 'but I have to go.' Terry and I exchange quizzical glances. Jones had distinctly promised us an hour. Only fifteen minutes have elapsed. The drummer starts putting on his coat and gathering up his things. As he does so, I throw him one last question.

Out and about on Westmoreland Terrace, Pimlico, circa 1966.

'Do you find it weird all this, having to remember events in your life that go back nearly thirty years now?'

'That's exactly what I was thinking,' he replies, sounding almost relieved. 'As I was reading the book I was thinking to myself, I really don't want to do this. Nothing against you, but as far as I'm concerned, the story is so sad. Look at The Small Faces. We started out as best of friends and had all that success. Yet we never made any money out of it and we fell out. The singer is now dead, the bass player is ill and the keyboard player lives far away in America. It's hard to think about it at all. I'll see you later.'

After he's gone, Terry swears he saw a tear in Jones's eye just before he went to the gents. We are left to sit in silence.

In so many ways, Jones is right. On one level, The Small Faces story is a classic tale of betrayal, music business corruption, divided loyalties, teenage friendships and unachieved ambitions.

It is the story of four close friends – Steve Marriott, Ronnie Lane, Ian McLagan and Kenney Jones – entering the pop world with bags of talent and attitude, and being driven apart by success and ego. Their first mistake was to become pop stars overnight. Their second was an inability to resist adding humour to so many of their records. And their third was never to play in America.

Not only did each of these factors cruelly ensure that they were never taken as seriously as their contemporaries, such as The Beatles or The Rolling Stones, but each one also drove the most forceful member, Steve Marriott, out of the band.

Yet undeniably the group helped to shape and influence the sixties, pop music's most important decade, as much as anyone else. Furthermore, that influence still lives and breathes, gathering momentum and providing each successive generation with a real sense of motivation and inspiration – Led Zeppelin, The Jam and Mother Earth are but three examples. Their look, attitude and unerring ability to make their records compelling slices of musical intensity and action means that their work speaks as directly now as it did back in the sixties.

The Small Faces existed, barring an ill-advised comeback in the mid-1970s, for a brief, explosive four years. Within that period they made records that were so complete that when you listened to them nothing but the music seemed to matter – the hallmark of great art.

It was through this body of work that The Small Faces became key but hidden figures in the transformation of British pop from light entertainment to an art form that demanded to be taken seriously. Along with a like-minded team of musicians, they put energy, passion, sex, intelligence and style into pop and set an example for everyone to come.

The Small Faces were one of the sixties' quintessential pop groups. As teenagers, they were exactly the right age when stardom hit them and, as authentic East End Mods, they always looked the part: sharp, dynamic, not one detail out of place. The Small Faces were Mod incarnate. The clothes

and the haircuts, combined with their fresh-faced innocence, created a look that was not only the epitome of their era but which still, nearly thirty years later, carries great resonance. There were other authentic Mod bands – The Action, The Creation – but the prolific nature of Marriott and Lane, coupled with the band's ability to survive under the heat and pressure of sixties' stardom, ensured that The Small Faces rose to the top and stayed there. Maybe they believed in Modernism just that little bit more.

It's a cliché in today's cynical and hardbitten times, but The Small Faces really did start out with little more in mind than fun and the avoidance of the factory line to which so many of their class were doomed. Three had played skiffle music as youngsters, two had already appeared on records. They had all been in unsuccessful groups and, when they finally came together, they had lost the initial illusion of instant pop stardom that is the preserve of hungry young musicians. All they wanted was a giggle and a smile and that, their leader Steve

Rare shot of Marriott's short-lived moustache.

11

'Young people are desperately unhappy doing jobs they don't like and now they are asking, why should we? I was unhappy in the factory where I worked. During your lifetime you went through two World Wars and there wasn't much time to think about things. But now there is and the chance to do something about it.'

'But you're an exception. You've worked hard and you've got talent. Most kids don't even want to entertain themselves today or anyone else.'

'You only think that because I'm your son. The milkman could have done what I've done if he had wanted to know and made the effort.'

RONNIE LANE, TALKING WITH HIS FATHER,
OCTOBER 1967

Marriott once explained, was the reason they were so successful.

When they played together, a certain magic became discernible to anyone who was listening. All four were so in tune with the others' playing that the music flowed naturally. They truly brought out the best in each other.

Steve Marriott, talking about the art of songwriting and how their music was created, once said in a Radio One interview, 'It might be pouring out of Ronnie or it might be pouring out of me, but if there's someone there to egg you on, stem the flow, and give you little tangents to go on, that's more writing together than actually sitting down and saying, "Right, now what have you got?"'

Kenney Jones adds, 'We were all free to do what we wanted and we were all sensitive to each other's playing.'

The Small Faces had five basic musical styles to call upon: R & B, pop, psychedelia, folk and the music hall tradition they were exposed to as children growing up in London's East End. Their genius was to mix these diverse elements into brilliant pop music and then top it with arrangements that were

'At the moment we are trying to find a sound of our own. We want people to recognise us immediately. But we don't want to do this by copying anyone else.'

KENNEY JONES, OCTOBER 1965

Ian McLagan on *Ready Steady Go*. His organ playing was a vital part of The Small Faces sound.

Classic snap of the band, circa 1966.

unique, a sound which was as raw as the streets on which they were raised.

As Mod teenagers they also listened to much of the imported and hard-to-get American R & B records that were being played at the clubs they often frequented. Acts such as Booker T and the MGs, Ray Charles and Bobby Bland were not only the purveyors of the essential Mod soundtrack, they also served to persuade Marriott and Lane, especially, of the value of soul.

It was partly this quest – to match the emotional intensity of these artists but in their own distinct manner – that not only formed the basis of some of The Small Faces' best records but directly helped lay a musical tradition of British groups playing Black American R & B, a tradition which is stronger than ever today. Unlike many of their contemporaries, The Small Faces sought not to clean up the R & B sound but to dirty it even further. After they were finished with songs such as 'Every Little Bit Hurts' or 'Shake' they would tell their admirers to forget their version and buy the real thing. They were fans first, pop stars second. Musicians who retain the thrill of being moved by music will always last the longest.

In their chief musical directors, Steve Marriott and Ronnie Lane, they had two class songwriters. In turn Jones and McLagan, the latter himself an occasional writer, were the perfect musicians to realise in full their musical aims. That they all stood under five foot three was just part of the destiny that they all suspected existed but were at a loss to articulate. Their coming together was both mystical and magical.

'If people are bugged about their size I have some advice for them: put a load of manure underneath the bed and after a couple of days you'll find a remarkable difference.'

RONNIE LANE, AUGUST 1966

Steve Marriott, in Kenney Jones's words, 'was a ball of energy and fun', and it was this spirit which infused the band from the outset. Success and its attendant pressures slowly strangled those smiles, and then drove the group apart.

That the band were close is an understatement. They knew each other intimately from the ages of about sixteen to twenty-three. They spent countless hours together, crammed into cars, vans, dressing rooms, TV studios, hotels and planes. They even shared a house together in Pimlico.

By the time they were making (but not receiving) big money, the group was a business, forced to hire accountants and lawyers and worry about grown-up matters – the very things from which they had tried

Lane contemplating the *Ready Steady Go* audience.

to escape. It killed their innocence, with Steve Marriott perhaps the first to feel it.

Marriott may have looked easy to assess from the outside – the incorrigible working-class Cockney with the Cor Blimey expressions – but inside was a restless artist who became bored quickly and always wanted to move on. He was a complex, private man who couldn't help but dominate any public arena he was in, be it studio, stage or socially. For many people, his larger-than-life persona was too much to take.

He was also confused about his talents. On the one hand he desperately wanted to be taken as seriously as the other top bands of the time, like The Rolling Stones, with whom he occasionally fraternised. On the other, he was fond of professing that he was only in it for a good time. He believed, and rightly so, that his music was as inventive as anything else coming out of Britain at that time, but when he finally achieved his goal, with the band's acclaimed *Ogdens' Nut Gone Flake* album, his

insecurities surfaced and he convinced himself he could go no further.

It badly hurt him that the band's rough-and-tumble image, their humour and their lack of pretension, camouflaged so much of their work. It is only now, as time clears away prejudices, that we see Marriott and Lane as the great songwriters they truly were.

In Ronnie Lane, Marriott had the perfect partner. While you would expect Marriott to be at the centre of the action, Lane always seemed a little withdrawn, a little detached. He too hated the trappings of pop stardom and the way it distorted their musical ambitions. Like Marriott, Lane was a tough little East Ender, but he was also a romantic at heart. The bright lights soon meant very little to him.

Their long-time engineer and co-producer, Glyn Johns, says of the two, 'They were very different characters. Marriott was far more openly aggressive than Ronnie and that came out in his music and the way he played his guitar. Ronnie was much more of a romantic, a bit of a softie really. Later on he got into Meher Baba and all that. Steve Marriott would never have gotten into anything like that. He wouldn't have wanted to bare his soul like that. He wouldn't want anyone looking in. He would rather bluff his way through by aggression, keep everybody at arm's length.'

The other two members were harder to figure out. Ian McLagan always appeared slightly mysterious, a little bit elsewhere, while Kenney Jones had a hard but angelic look, which he still retains.

Yet put them together in front of a camera and they were perfect, an entity, a unit that moved with true purpose.

As teenagers in the sixties, they grew up at a time when the working class were afforded more opportunities in the arts than ever before. In music The Beatles, four working-class Liverpudlians, had shown the way by writing their own material and inciting hysteria on a scale seldom witnessed before or since. Michael Caine in film and David Bailey in photography had also made important breakthroughs.

The creation of the teenager, with disposable income and a thirst for freedom, never before experienced by British society, had produced a demand to which the arts, especially pop music, responded immediately. The Small Faces were a vital part of that process.

They had a healthy air of arrogance and cynicism and, above all, an insatiable drive to make music that was not only dynamic and forceful but which attempted both to extend and to define pop's boundaries. In this respect, The Small Faces caught the artistic spirit of their times.

Much of the sixties, especially the years in which The Small Faces existed, was a time of vast social upheaval. Values that had never been questioned were now being fiercely attacked and very few institutions were left unscathed. All pillars of society were challenged and found wanting, especially if their only response was brute force. Authority was no longer accepted or acceptable. Change was in the air and that invisible force swept across America and Europe.

In the US that meant, among other things, the Civil Rights movement, the protest against Vietnam, the assassinations of John F. Kennedy, Malcolm X and Martin Luther King, urban ghetto riots, the hippie movement, Woodstock and, finally, the drug-crazed hell that was Altamont.

In Britain, the Profumo scandal of 1963 (where a leading MP, John Profumo, first denied and then admitted sexual liaisons with society girl Christine Keeler) brought down the government and paved the way for the start of 'The Sixties' and 'Swinging London'.

The arrival of biting satirical TV programmes such as *That Was The Week That Was* (which was forced off the air in the election year of 1966), plus an alternative and very influential underground press, the wide use of drugs, the sexual revolution and the student protest movement, all served to establish a heady air of freedom. Traditionally, and as part of its function, pop music responded to these forces, albeit in an unconscious form.

The response from songwriters such as Lennon and McCartney, Bob Dylan, Jagger and Richards, Pete Townshend and Ray Davies, not to mention ground-breaking labels such as Stax, Atlantic and Motown, was fierce and intense. With each new

Kenney Jones on *Ready Steady Go*.

record there seemed to be a new sound, a new style, another step forward. As society changed, so did its music. The Small Faces were never political but their work easily survived the heat. On nearly every one of their records there is a sense of invention and a search for something new.

The proof of their success is that nearly thirty years on their records still move with a kick and passion that is unique. Small Faces music does not date.

Their early image as teen pop idols and working-class Mods often caused this vibrant artistic side to be overlooked. It was only with *Ogdens' Nut Gone Flake* and its revolutionary packaging and 'concept' that serious critical acclaim began to come their way. But by then it was too late. Unable to play their masterwork live, within seven months of the LP's release the group was effectively finished.

Not that success had eluded them too much. Eleven of their fourteen singles had reached top

15

thirty status. Two had missed completely, while their last offering on 45 rpm, 'Afterglow (Of Your Love)'/'Wham Bam Thank You Mam', had peaked at thirty-six. Their three official LP releases had gone top twenty, with *Ogdens' Nut Gone Flake* staying at number one in the UK charts for six weeks.

Overseas they were equally, if not more, successful. The group were probably bigger in Germany than they were in the UK, while in America 'Itchycoo Park' gave them a number-two single and their only US success.

Despite this, the group never succumbed to self-importance or pretentiousness. They had too much energy and style to fall into that trap. They might have laughed at the machinations of the pop world but they never forgot to put themselves down.

They came together in 1965 to begin a career that was often characterised by arguments and frustration – with their management, the authorities, the media, their record companies and, though it was never overtly stated, their audience. They were managed by two of the sixties' most flamboyant managers, Don Arden and Andrew Loog Oldham, and yet, throughout their many tribulations, they maintained an impish demeanour.

In Steve Marriott, they had a vocalist of outstanding quality, arguably one of the ten best British voices to have emerged in the last three decades. He based his vocals on singers such as Ray Charles, James Brown and Muddy Waters, and acquitted himself with flying colours. To hear him sing 'Every Little Bit Hurts', to name but one example, was to hear a vocal performance of exceptional quality and authenticity, a display of emotional power that only the very best could surpass.

The group possessed a devil-may-care attitude that undoubtedly hampered their career chances in the conventional sense but spoke volumes for their refusal to compromise their values. The Small Faces took drugs, annoyed crucial music business figures, created havoc from here to Australia and happily assisted the careers of artists as diverse as P. P. Arnold, Chris Farlowe and French singer Johnny Hallyday.

It was this integrity that was another important factor in their appeal and an underlying reason for the force of their records. They would not, as far as they could, compromise their artistic impulses or their determination to have fun for anyone, be it their audience or record company. Similarly, as working-class boys who knew only too well the drudgery and pain of nine-to-five work, they resisted becoming a factory-line product themselves.

The result was that The Small Faces left behind a series of records that are genuine pop masterpieces, songs that will remain timeless. They not only offer a blueprint for all aspiring musicians but, in their chequered and colourful career, provide a story that is the epitome of pop history.

Which is why, some twenty-odd years after Steve Marriott threw down his guitar and stalked off stage at Alexandra Palace, thus extinguishing the band, they deserve to be celebrated and restored to their rightful position.

It is our hope that this book will be part of that process.

Paolo Hewitt, May 1994

Steve Marriott, circa 1967.

16

Classic Gered Mankowitz shot from 1968.

Marriott as a teenager, hungry for success.

ALL OUR YESTERDAYS

Are you sitting four square comfty bubble? Then we'll begin.

Each member of The Small Faces was born within three years of the end of the Second World War into an austere food-rationed Britain. Three – Steve Marriott, Ronnie Lane and Kenney Jones – came from London's infamous East End, while their keyboard player, Ian McLagan, hailed from Hounslow, Middlesex.

Of the four, Stephen Peter Marriott's childhood was easily the most eventful. Born on 30 January 1947, in East Ham Memorial Hospital, to Bill and Kathleen Marriott, Steve was first raised at 26 Strone Road, Manor Park. The road is in fact opposite the Ruskin Arms pub, the site for the first Small Faces rehearsals. (A certain David Cook, who would one day change his surname to Essex, lived a couple of doors away.) Five years later Steve's sister Kay was born.

At a very early age, Marriott displayed great enthusiasm for music. His passion was so evident that his father bought him a ukelele and gave him

basic lessons. Later on, the family formed a skiffle group around their son and would go out on to their street to give impromptu concerts for the neighbours – an example of the kind of encouragement and love that his parents showered upon him, thus bestowing him with the necessary confidence to face the world from a stage.

But the performing didn't stop there. Marriott would often take his instrument and busk outside the local cemetery gates, entertaining the people queuing at the nearby bus stop. At other times, accompanied by his Aunt Joan, he would visit local old people's homes and perform for the residents there. By all accounts he was a huge Buddy Holly fan.

As well as a separate passion for animals, which he never lost, Marriott's fixation with music meant that at twelve, when he was enrolled in Sandringham Secondary Modern School in Manor Park, he showed little aptitude for the school curriculum, save Drama.

Given his inclinations to perform, it was no surprise when his mum and Aunt Sheila (who both worked as secretaries for music publishers) spotted an ad in the *Daily Mirror* inviting applicants to audition for the part of the Artful Dodger in a stage production of *Oliver!*. They insisted that Steve apply.

On the given day, a very young and nervous Steve Marriott was taken to the audition by his father, where he performed Buddy Holly's 'Oh Boy'. The show's director, Lionel Bart, who remembered Marriott from his East End busking stints, gave him the job. It was the start of a public career that would

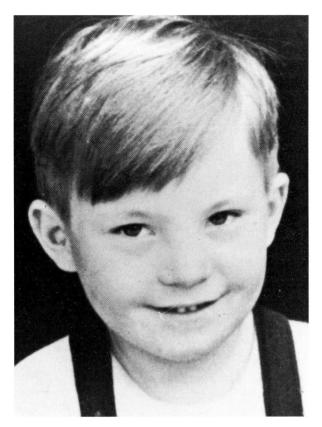 

Top left: Marriott aged four. War is over but his teeth have yet to appear. Top right: On holiday in Clacton.

separate Marriott from his school contemporaries. Every night bar Sundays, for the next fourteen months, Marriott appeared in the show. It was through this engagement that he made his recording debut – on the stagecast album, *Oliver!*. His thin, youthful vocals can be heard on 'Consider Yourself', 'Be Back Soon' and 'I'd Do Anything'.

Though he was still obliged to attend school, Marriott saw no reason to when he was working every night and he literally went on strike, attending even fewer lessons. This pointless inactivity ceased the day Marriott dropped a lit cigarette down a hole in the floor at school. 'We used to smoke in the woodwork class,' Marriott once recalled, 'and shove the butts down a knot hole in the floor. Well, I kicked mine down it and it must have caught a gas main because a two-foot flame shot up it.'

Marriott's actions not only made the *Stratford Express*, under the headline LITTLE CHICAGO BURNS, with a picture of the perpetrator dressed as the Artful Dodger, but also led to him heading for the

'I couldn't concentrate and ended up being more or less expelled. For burning the school down! It was an accident. I got bored during a lesson and was mucking about. Dropped a lighted match through a hole in the floor. I thought it would go out but it struck a gas pipe and the place went up.'

STEVE MARRIOTT, SEPTEMBER 1966

Italia Conti drama school in Islington, following a mutual agreement between Marriott's parents and the headmaster of his now badly scorched school.

Marriott was to spend two years at this prestigious drama school. To pay for his tuition he took every job offered to him. At fourteen, he landed his first television role in *Mr Pastry*, before going on to work with Sid James in *Citizen James*, Jack Warner in *Dixon of Dock Green* (Marriott played a street kid who shoots his mum) and Eric Sykes and Peter Sellers in the film *Heaven's Above*.

On the set of this film, in which Marriott played the elder child of a family taken in by Peter Sellers' vicar, Marriott, Sellers and Sykes whiled away the

Stephen picks pockets—once nightly

HERE'S the story of a boy Jekyll and Hyde . . . a shaggy - haired 14 - year - old who leaves his neat council home every evening to join London's worst g a n g of juvenile cut-throats!

He's just a normal boy to teachers in class C3A at Manor Park's Sandringham school. Pocket-sized Stephen Marriott likes swimming, billiards, table tennis and English . . . and hates maths.

But five hours after school he's dressed in ragged trousers, down-at-heel shoes and a slouch hat.

Stephen's a pickpocket . . . one of the 14-strong gang which nightly delights West End audiences in Lionel Bart's hit " Oliver."

"There's always something different going on," he says. " I love it. I want to go on the stage when I leave school."

A few months ago Stephen, of Daines-close, Manor Park, wanted to be a groom or a vet.

But he forgot all that one night when his mother told him:

" You're going to audition for a West End musical tomorrow ! "

She wrote to Lionel Bart when she heard he was looking for youngsters for the workhouse and thieves' kitchen scenes.

Stephen—who is met every night from the theatre by mum or dad—earns £8 a week.

A third of that is put away and he's buying a new guitar.

And although he says the show has taught him " quite a few pick-pocket tricks" he's quite happy with his work.

One of Marriott's first press cuttings from the *Stratford Express*, 1961.

hours by forming a ukelele group and entertaining the film's crew and cast.

After completing *Heaven's Above,* work began to dry up a little. Marriott wasn't too bothered as the long hours spent waiting around on sets had bored him. Music seemed a far more exciting prospect. On impulse, he decided to swap acting for playing music. As he had just been asked to join the prestigious Old Vic Company for a six-month run in Chichester, his decision threw him into conflict with his parents. Determined to see their son pursue an acting career, they thought it madness to throw away such a golden opportunity.

The resulting friction caused the sixteen-year-old Marriott to leave home for a while, living at various addresses, including his Aunt Sheila's and a bedsit in Finsbury Park. Although the family would soon be reunited, the incident speaks volumes on Marriott's stubborn streak.

The group he eventually formed was called The Moonlighters. They specialised in Shadows covers but failed to gain any meaningful recognition, and

'You see, it was this acting thing. My parents were dead keen on it and I was doing pretty well. They couldn't see why it wasn't enough for me. I had a bug about groups, always had been dead keen on music. For me acting wasn't absorbing, it was boring. All that hanging about.'

STEVE MARRIOTT, SEPTEMBER 1966

soon folded. After this initial failure, Marriott, through his Aunt Sheila's connections, reluctantly returned to film work.

His next role was in a typical 'Swinging Sixties' beat movie entitled *Live It Up* (Rank, 1963). The lead parts were assigned to David Hemmings and Heinz Burt (who later dropped the surname, played on the Tornados' massive hit record 'Telstar' and then scored a 1963 chart record with his Eddie Cochran tribute 'Just Like Eddie'), while Marriott played the role of a drummer called Ricky.

The plot revolved around a group recording a demo of their song 'Live It Up'. The tape then gets lost. Following a series of madcap adventures the

At his parents' holiday home in Jaywick Sands, 1958.

tape is found and it's smiles all round. A point of interest: the music for the film, which was supplied by such disparate acts as Gene Vincent, Kenny Ball's Jazzmen and Sounds Incorporated, was produced by Joe Meek, a seminal British producer whose unique sound revolutionised early production values.

Steve's next role was in the sequel, *Be My Guest* (Rank, 1963), which basically followed the same route as its predecessor, only this time the band enter a talent contest. The film's title refers to the song they demo and have stolen.

Shel Talmy, who would go on to work with The Who and The Yardbirds, produced the music while Jerry Lee Lewis and The Nashville Teens are among the acts featured. The lengthy process of making these two films was finally enough to convince the restless Marriott that he should follow his instincts and go back to music.

In 1964 he landed a short-lived job playing harmonica with The Andrew Oldham Orchestra (Oldham was at that time looking after a young Rolling Stones and would later manage The Small Faces) before striking out on his own and forming his first group, The Frantics.

The band was more in keeping with Marriott's musical tastes. Although they were obliged to perform covers of recent hits, as groups were in those days, they also incorporated into their repertoire covers of the imported American R & B tunes that were increasingly catching Marriott's attention.

These kinds of number complimented Marriott's new lifestyle as a Mod, a secretive cult that was slowly gaining favour with the capital's youth. Mods were the complete antithesis of the fifties' Teddy Boy style which had arrived in Britain via the music of Elvis Presley and the imagery of James Dean and Marlon Brando. Mods favoured sharp tailored clothes over the dirty jeans and leather jackets, Black American R & B music over rock 'n' roll, cappuccino and pills over beer, and scooters over Harley Davidsons. At the centre of their self-contained world, a cool look and attitude was paramount.

'Clothes to us were essential,' Marriott once told me. 'I don't know why, it's hard to put into words. It was a case of all me mates were Mods and I was a Mod . . . Like we'd take pills, stay up all night. It was the Scene Club until midnight, then the Flamingo for the all-nighter. It was being sick in alleyways, ruining the jacket you just payed an arm and a leg for. I just thought everything was marvellous.'

Modernism had begun in the late fifties. Its birthplace was London's East End so it's no surprise that Marriott took to it. The roots of Modernism are hard to trace but many ascribe the presence of American soldiers stationed in Britain, with their penchant for sharp suits and modern jazz, as the catalyst for the movement. One only has to look at the superbly moody pictures of Miles Davis circa 1958, dressed in a Brook Brothers suit, to see the connection.

Modernism would not make its way into the national consciousness until 1964 when the media latched on to stories of Mods fighting rockers at seaside resorts like Clacton, Margate and Brighton, sensationally splashing them all over the front pages.

Once it went overground, the movement lost its central point. Unlike their sworn enemies, the detested rockers, the Mods adopted a secret rebellious stance. They had to work. Money was crucial

Press shot from the film *Live It Up*. Marriott's grin caught on celluloid.

to sustaining the lifestyle. Subsequently, Mods took great pleasure in dressing smarter than their bosses and blending in with the rest of their square co-workers. By day they seemed 'normal' kids. At night, and especially at weekends, their intake of pills and their club-hopping behaviour would have scandalised their superiors.

With fashion changing every week, Mods had to be able to keep up. To go out dressed in an item that was considered passé was to invoke humiliation. Along with the all-important clothes, there were also the American R & B records to buy, a scooter to maintain, and money for the weekend's activities, which would start Friday night and carry through until Sunday evening.

The Mod philosophy was about staying one step ahead of everyone around you, whether that be your boss, whose dowdy suit and tie you would snigger at behind his back, or your friends, whom you would try to outdo with the latest fashions.

The Frantics, with their R & B numbers, can now be seen as Marriott's first attempt to reflect the Mod ethic through a group. He also changed the band's name and, in an early show of self-confidence, started the Steve Marriott and the Moments fan club, which was run by Ann Marshall.

Included in the group's line-up was Kenny Rowe on bass, Sean Buckley on guitar and Vin Nicholls on drums. These four formed the nucleus of the group, with other musicians floating in and out. Vin Nicholls states that one of these loose members was Jimmy Winston, The Small Faces' first organ player although Marriott never confirmed or made mention of this in any interview. Among the songs they played were Arthur Alexander's 'Anna', The Beatles' 'I Saw Her Standing There' and the Coasters' 'Love Potion Number Nine'.

The group were on the books of the Clayman agency, who found them gigs at places such as the Dover Castle in Stepney, the Albion in Rainham, the Robert Clack Youth Centre in Dagenham, and the Magnet and Dewdrop (a transvestite hang-out in the Isle of Dogs). The agency also managed to secure them a regular spot at the Thingandmejig Club in Reading.

In 1964 the group signed to Decca and recorded a version of The Kinks' "You Really Got Me', with 'Money, Money' (by D. Charles and A. Caddie) as the B-side. The record was turned down by Decca but taken up by the World Artists label, an American company. The single was released in the US only as a blatant attempt to cash in before The Kinks could

The mean and moody look for the struggling actor.

release their original version there. The record quickly disappeared and soon after Steve quit the group.

'The Moments,' he later recalled, 'were a great band, always had great guitarists. We got John Weider [who would go on to join The Animals] later on. He was my age or a bit younger but the rest were older than me and all were better musicians than me. All I did was fuck about on piano, play a bit of harmonica and sing. Aside from demos nothing was really happening so they got despondent and kicked me out to get a better singer, another boy they knew who was five years older than me. I don't really blame them.'

In the early sixties, many bands were formed but few were chosen. It was the teenager's impossible dream to make a record. Compared with today, very few British bands were allowed through the doors of major record companies, companies which, as we shall see, were run by people who had no idea whatsoever about their audience or the emerging importance of pop music. But releasing a record, albeit in another country, was more than enough encouragement for Marriott to begin writing his own material.

To find an outlet for it, he hit upon the idea of trying Tin Pan Alley, in reality Soho's Denmark Street, whose buildings were then filled with music publishers. Marriott spent the day turning up unannounced at various offices only to be denied entry. It was then that his Aunt Sheila again stepped in to help him out. She told her boss, music publisher Jack Hylton, of her nephew's ambitions, and through his contacts Marriott landed an appointment with a publisher called Franklin Boyd. On the given day, Marriott showed up at Boyd's office and played him 'Imaginary Love', his own composition.

Boyd liked the song but, more importantly, loved Marriott's voice. He phoned Decca Records and within two weeks Steve Marriott recorded his debut solo single.

'Give Her My Regards' was a Kenny Lynch composition backed with Marriott's own 'Imaginary Love'. An eternal optimist, Marriott was convinced the single would bring him the recognition he so badly sought. He was wrong.

The single bombed, leaving Marriott without film or recording work. (Later in life, Marriott would mention a second solo single, produced by Andrew Loog Oldham, a cover of The Rolling Stones' 'Tell Me' coupled with Timi Yuro's 'Maybe'. However at the time of writing both Decca and Tony Calder, Loog Oldham's partner, deny any knowledge of this single. It could well be that a version was made but rejected by Decca and exists only in demo form.)

With no income Marriott had no other option but to take a Saturday job at the J60 music shop in his homeground of Manor Park. It was there that one day two young Mods came in to enquire about a bass guitar. Marriott vaguely recognised both of them but history does not record if he noticed the striking similarities between all three of them. All were Mods, all were small and all were aspiring musicians.

One of the young Mods standing in front of Marriott that day was Ronald Frederick Lane, born on 1 April 1946, in Plaistow, East London, to Stanley and Elsie Lane.

'I had a wonderful childhood,' Lane states. 'I had the best dad in the world. His name was Stan Stanley and he looked after us kids pretty good although he was poor. He was a truck driver. I have a brother who, in the tradition, was also called Stan.'

When he was five years old, Lane made his first

Ronnie Lane as cowboy.

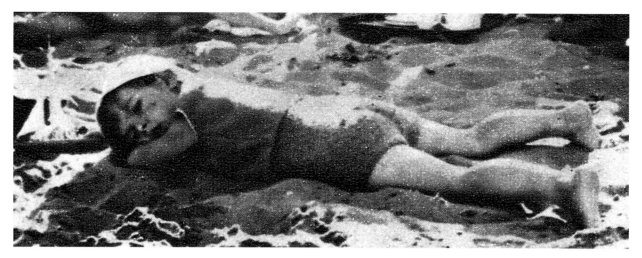

'I'm only dreaming.' Ronnie Lane sunbathes.

public appearance. Like Steve Marriott, it was as a busker playing the ukelele (a baby pink one in this case), singing cowboy songs for London Transport workers as they changed shifts. Again like Marriott, Lane detested school. 'I got into a lot of fights and got picked on a lot because I was small. I didn't like lessons much and I was not interested in sport. When we had games I did the odd jobs like oiling the tennis posts.'

At fourteen, Lane, a big fan of instrumental bands such as The Shadows, began playing guitar, and at sixteen he quit school to enroll in an art course at the Lister Technical College. By now, he was a fully-fledged Mod.

'There was nothing else to do,' he recalls. 'That was all that was happening at the time. I didn't want to be a greasy rocker, did I?'

Lane also joined the Green Jackets Rifle Brigade where, while out on manoeuvres, he briefly met a recruit from another unit named Kenney Jones.

But it was holiday work at the Battersea Fun Fair that would prove to be most auspicious. Lane landed a part-time job managing the Roll-A-Penny stall before moving on to work the Big Dipper. His fairground experiences were to leave an indelible mark on him and they would surface with regularity in his subsequent compositions. Lane loved every aspect of the fairground but it was the nomadic lifestyle of his co-workers that was to prove irresistible, and he soon quit college to work full-time at Battersea.

'My last task at the end of the season was remov-

ing the bulbs from the Big Dipper's girders,' Lane told author John Pidgeon. 'I nearly fell off the top of that a few times. The trouble with that job was that the season used to finish in September. You know, a fair when it's closed is the saddest sight in the world.'

When the season finished, Lane, who was reluctant to leave his family, headed home to form his first group, The Outcasts. He would later change the name to The Pioneers. The group's line-up included the brilliantly named Nogsy Newman on bass and a singer called George.

Just as bass players were in short supply around the East End, drummers were equally hard to find. Within a group, the bass and drums play the least glamorous roles both musically and publicly. Everyone wants to be out front. Lane's problem was finding someone willing to take a back seat and provide good enough instrumentation.

By chance, Stan, Ronnie's barman brother, had spotted a young drummer who would occasionally play with his pub's regular band. A meeting was arranged and Kenney Jones walked in. This time he and Lane were out of uniform and spent the time discussing and enthusing about music. Both were big Shadows fans and Lane offered Jones a position in the band.

Despite an argument with the other members, who preferred another drummer, Lane prevailed and Jones became a fully-fledged member.

The Pioneers' non existent income at the time

meant that Lane was forced to take on a variety of soul-destroying jobs. These included delivering false teeth for a dentist, working in a gentlemen's outfitters (where he hit a salesman over the head with a window pole) and acting as a pipefitter's helper. It was some months before he finally landed a job that he not only found acceptable but which was also to prove crucial to his musical development: testing amplifiers for Selmer's.

'They wheeled in the amps,' Lane told Pidgeon. 'You plugged it in and played, and if it worked you chucked it out and if it didn't you chucked it back down the line again.

'So that was when I started fucking about with the bass in my dinner hour. And it was such a bastard down the East End to get a bass player, I thought, I don't mind being a fucking bass player. I quite liked it. I was getting very involved with Booker T and the MGs at the time and I liked that approach of, "It's not what you play, it's what you don't play."'

As in Marriott's case, it was a musical decision that would cause friction within the Lane family. His father had recently signed a hire purchase agreement for his son's guitar. Now he wanted to switch to bass. How could he pay for both? Eventually Lane settled the argument. He agreed to pay the instalments on the first guitar while pointing out that with a bass 'At least I can get some fuckin' work in a band because there ain't no bass players.'

The next step was to acquire a bass guitar – which is why Ronnie Lane and Kenney Jones took a trip down to the J60 music shop in Green Lanes, Manor Park, to find a suitable instrument.

When they walked in both Jones and Lane thought they knew Marriott. According to him, they had actually seen him at a Moments gig the year before in Rainham, Essex, when they had supported his group and been totally outclassed.

'It was the first time we had come across Steve,' Jones recalls of that day at the music shop. 'But I recognised his face straightaway. He was already playing regularly with other bands from the area. But that wasn't where I knew him from. I just couldn't place him, it was like I dreamt I knew him.'

While Jones tried to figure out why he recognised the young shop assistant, Lane and Marriott struck

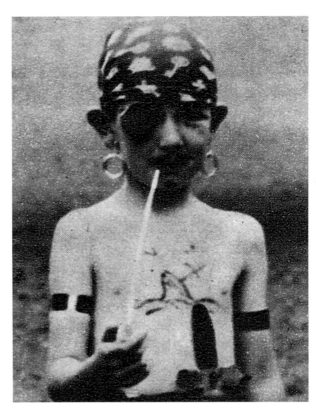
Early shot of Ronnie Lane on holiday.

up an instant rapport. Lane talked about his influences, groups such as Booker T and the MGs, while Marriott enthused over his musical loves, artists such as the bluesman Bobby Bland.

'And then,' recalls Jones, 'we set up some instruments and, much to the annoyance of the other customers, we spent the afternoon jamming. I remember thinking that Steve was really friendly and a real ball of fun.'

When the shop closed for the day, Marriott invited Lane back to his house. That night he played him a selection of his record collection, including tracks by artists such as Muddy Waters, Ray Charles and Charlie and Innez Fox. For Lane it was a revelation. He was inspired by the music. He also liked Marriott: both were Mods and both shared the same sense of humour. (In fact, it was Marriott who gave Lane his lifelong nickname of 'Plonk'. He bestowed it upon him after hearing Lane's early efforts on the guitar, which, by all accounts, were even more limited than Marriott's own.)

A few weeks later, the friendship having been cemented by Marriott selling Lane a Harmony bass at far below the asking price, Ronnie invited Steve down to the Earl of Derby pub in Grange Road, Bermondsey, to jam with his group. It would prove to be a memorable evening.

The Earl of Derby was important to The Pioneers. It was one of the very few places where they were assured of regular work. After Marriott's debut appearance with them this would no longer be the case.

'We started drinking whiskies,' Lane told Pidgeon. 'First time I'd ever really drunk any and there was this false sense of bravado going on about how much the pair of us could put back. In the end we got totally pissed.'

The result was total mayhem. Halfway through a set of pale Searchers covers, Marriott got bored and started hammering on the piano, Jerry Lee Lewis style. Within minutes, he had literally demolished the piano.

'So we all got the bullet,' Lane recalls, 'and of course my name was shit because I'd brought this character down the pub and blown a really good gig.'

It was that night, too, that Jones finally figured out where he knew Marriott from. 'It was when we went round to pick him up for the gig that it dawned on me where I'd seen him before,' Jones recalls. 'I realised I'd seen him in those films. It was like, I know who you are. So we said to the audience that night, "We've got this very special guest for you," winding them up, thinking they would all know Steve Marriott, which, of course, nobody did.'

Kenneth Thomas Jones was born on 16 September 1948 in Stepney, London, to Violet and Samuel Jones. His first secondary school was St George's In The East, Cable Street. Jones remembers it as 'a really tough school. I also hated it because all my mates were at the Dempsey Street School.'

To get around the absence of his friends, Jones would cycle to school and register his name. He would then sneak out, hop back on to his bicycle and ride over to Dempsey's.

'I would just choose the lessons I liked,' he recalls, 'things like metalwork and woodwork and do them, as well as hanging out with my friends. All the teachers thought I was a new boy.'

Early childhood pic of Kenney Jones.

When he was thirteen, Jones' musical interest began in earnest. One afternoon, as he and his mate were washing a mutual friend's car for the princely sum of 2/6d, his companion suggested that they form a skiffle group, a popular thing to do at the time.

The success of skiffle acts like Lonnie Donegan, who hit big in 1956 with his song 'Rock Island Line', as well as the growing reputation of bars such as the Two I's, where acts such as Marty Wilde and Tommy Steele and The Caveman were making a name for themselves playing this type of music, had persuaded many budding musicians that skiffle was the easiest route to success.

The equipment needed was cheap and basic and much of it could be made at home. This included two acoustic guitars, a banjo, drums played with brushes, a stand-up bass or a broom handle placed in a tea chest with one string to pluck, and even combs and washboards to heighten the effect.

Furthermore, added Jones's friend, there was a

skiffle act on TV that night. They could watch them and pick up ideas.

'So me and my mate went home and watched this act and it was Lonnie Donegan,' Jones recalls. 'I actually fell in love with the sound of the banjo, that was the instrument I wanted to play.'

Soon after, Jones went down to a second-hand shop in Bethnal Green where his friend had seen a cheap banjo for sale. He was too late, it had already been sold. He returned home and told his friend who said not to worry, he had a drum kit he would bring down.

'It was one drum and a couple of cymbals,' Jones recalls, 'but after I started playing around on it I really liked it.' To further his new-found interest, Jones went to the J60 music shop in Manor Park and spotted a white Olympic kit. The asking price was sixty-four pounds, nine shillings and five pence. After enquiring about hire purchase terms, the owner told Jones he would need ten pounds for the deposit.

'So I went home to see my parents about it but

both of them were out. Only my mum's purse was in. So I took a tenner, went back to the shop and paid the deposit. Then the guy told me he could deliver it that night but he would need both my parents' signatures as I was too young to get it on HP.'

An apprehensive Jones returned home and waited. He didn't say a word to his parents about his purchase or where the money for the deposit had come from. At 7.15 p.m. the drum kit arrived.

'My dad, who knew nothing about this, opened the door and the guy came straight in thinking everything was cool. He set it up, got the brushes out and played a jazz kind of thing on the cymbals. Then he said, "Right, it's your turn." I thought, no, I'll never be able to do it. So I got behind the kit, closed my eyes and tried to play what he had just played. After what seemed like an eternity I started playing this beat. My parents by then could see how much I was into it so they signed the papers and I got my first drum kit.'

At the time, Jones watched a lot of TV and was constantly exposed to the pop music of the time. He became a big admirer of The Shadows and would play along to his parents' two 78 rpm records – '12th Street Rag' and the theme from Rawhide. 'I never want to hear those records again,' he says.

Another friend, Jimmy, played guitar and shared Jones' passion for The Shadows. The two of them would get together and run through as many Shadows tunes as they could. Not long after, they spotted an advert requiring a drummer and a guitarist for a band that was performing in a club in Swallow Street, Piccadilly.

'So we turned up and it was the owner's son's group. We auditioned and we were terrible. About a week later we got a really nice letter from the owner thanking us for coming down and even though we didn't get the job, he wrote, "Kenney Jones will go far." I've never forgotten that.'

Around this time, at the age of fifteen, Kenney had started sneaking into the British Prince pub in Stepney. He would surreptitiously order half a lager and spend the night watching the resident drummer. After about two weeks the drummer, clearly perturbed by Jones's staring, asked him why he kept looking at him all the time.

Kenney in the TA where he first met Ronnie.

Kenney with his first Olympic drum kit, bought on HP from the J60 music shop.

'I told him I was a drummer and wanted to pick up tips by watching him,' Jones explained. 'Next time I go in there, I'm standing at the bar when the drummer suddenly announces, "Ladies and gentlemen, tonight we have a special guest on drums," and I'm looking round to see who it is, and the guy says, "Kenney Jones!" Obviously, I was really scared and nervous but I got behind the kit and we went into some jazz number. That was the first time I played in a group where we were all in time. It was such a great feeling. I got such a buzz after it that I knew it was what I wanted to do.'

One of the barmen at the pub was Stan Lane who spoke to Jones after the gig and informed him that his younger brother, Ronnie, was forming a group. Would he be interested? Jones arranged to meet Ronnie at the pub the following week.

'I'll never forget meeting Ronnie Lane,' Jones enthuses. 'When he walked in the pub he looked like The Beatles before they did. He had on a grey suit, a really nice tie and I remember his collar was so starched that whenever he turned his head his neck looked like it was straight. It was hilarious.'

Unbeknown to Kenney, the group already had another drummer under consideration, 'A flash geezer who could do paradiddles. I was more steady and Ronnie wanted me in. The others went for this other guy but Ronnie said, "Bollocks, Kenney's in," and he forced me into the band.'

After Marriott's piano-smashing display at the Earl of Derby, The Pioneers' days were numbered. 'I got up the singer's [George's] nose a bit,' Marriott recalled. 'Like, I started to do a takeover bit. Because I can't help it. I'm an overwhelming kind of guy and that's something I have to live with. Anyway, we got on George's tits so much, especially me, that we decided to form a band and I decided I'd try to learn to play guitar properly if Ronnie would play bass.'

Lane then told Jones he was going along with Marriott and asked if he would come too. The drummer said yes. Between the three of them it was agreed that Marriott would move from keyboards and better himself on guitar. The trio then started to look around for a suitable keyboard player and

Kenney goes hop-picking.

Marriott remembered Jimmy Langwith (known as Jimmy Winston for all his public appearances), whom he knew from the J60 music shop.

'Jimmy Langwith used to come in,' Marriott said, 'and be particularly moody and, being quite impressionable, I quite dug him. I got to know him and started going down his mum and dad's pub called the Ruskin Arms.'

James Edward Winston Langwith was born in Stratford, East London, on 20 April 1945. He has two brothers, Frank and Derek. His parents, Bill and Cis Langwith, ran the Ruskin Arms in Manor Park while their son attended Stratford Green Secondary Modern. It was here that Langwith first started to learn the guitar, before later switching to piano.

In 1960, at the age of fifteen, he made his first public appearance at the Sunset Strip Club in Jersey, singing with a jazz band. A year later he met a TV producer who began to get him work in both film and television. Through this break, Jimmy became heavily involved in acting. He attended the E. Fifteen acting school, which is part of the Corbett Theatre in Loughton, Essex, and his subsequent acting career would see him chalk up some thirty film and TV appearances.

By all accounts, Winston's keyboard skills were very limited but his favourite connections allowed the rest of the group to overlook any shortcomings.

'There's the old tale,' Kenney Jones recalls, 'that Jimmy only got in the band because he had a van, an old Black Maria, which is basically true. But what's more to the point was that he lived in his parents' pub, which meant we had somewhere to play and rehearse, so the van was a bonus because his playing was terrible. Steve taught him a couple of notes which went da, da da da, da dah, which was "Everybody Needs Somebody To Love" by Solomon Burke. He got the flavour for it and went straight out and bought a huge Lesley cabinet, so he was in.'

Through his earlier musical efforts, Marriott had come into contact with Maurice King, The Walker Brothers's manager. It was through him that Marriott was able to book some free rehearsal time at King's Starlight Rooms in Paddington. King was tentatively interested in managing the group but, after hearing them rehearse, quickly put aside that idea.

The Small Faces then moved on to the Ruskin Arms, where they were guaranteed as much free rehearsal time as they needed. As they were starting to thrash about, another young keyboard player was beginning to make a name for himself.

Ian Patrick McLagan was born on 12 May 1945 in Hounslow, Middlesex, to Alec and Susan McLagan. (Later in life, The Small Faces's manager, Don Arden, added a year to his birthdate.)

McLagan grew up listening to early rock 'n' roll but didn't show too much aptitude for playing until his mum stepped in and bought him a piano. A frustrated pianist herself, she had decided that her

Ian McLagan as a child.

son would take the chance that she had thrown away. 'If Mum hadn't kept on at me,' he once said, 'I would have never learned the piano.'

McLagan attended the Spring Grove Grammar School in Isleworth, Middlesex, where, coincidentally, Tony Brainsby, who would later handle Small Faces publicity, was a fellow pupil.

At school McLagan proved himself good at long-distance running, 'Until I started smoking,' but hated most other subjects. He also disliked the piano lessons that his mum sent him to in Heathrow where, as the planes roared overhead, a teacher tried to put him through his paces.

'I hated practising scales so I would bunk off and

Totally Mod Marriott.

rave

APRIL 2s 6d

8 PAGE RAVER'S HOLIDAY GUIDE!
VOTE! VOTE! VOTE!
For Your RAVE!!
LOTS MORE
MONKEE
PICTURES!

rave

SETTING THE FASHION

AUGUST
2s 6d

THIS
IS A DUMMY.
EITHER SIDE IS A
SMALL FACE!
INSIDE THERE
ARE MORE
SMALL
FACES PLUS
WALKERS, BEATLES,
STONES, LATEST
BOY/GIRL FASHIONS

rave

NOVEMBER
2s 6d

HOW JOHN LENNON WON THE WAR! EXCLUSIVE PICTURES
RAVE DISCOTHEQUE FASHIONS
STEVE MARRIOTT RAVE-UP
THE LOOK-AGAIN BEAUTY LOOK

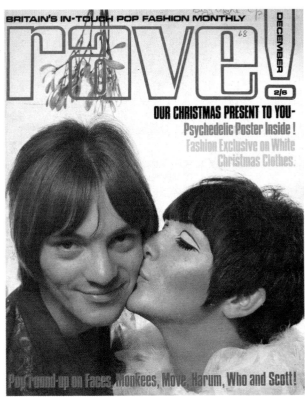

BRITAIN'S IN-TOUCH POP FASHION MONTHLY

rave!

DECEMBER
2/6

OUR CHRISTMAS PRESENT TO YOU—
Psychedelic Poster Inside !
Fashion Exclusive on White
Christmas Clothes.

Pop round-up on Faces, Monkees, Move, Harum, Who and Scott!

This page and opposite page top left and right: Such was the group's huge popularity, front covers were assured.

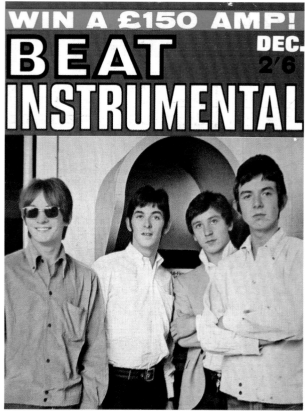

Above: Silly photos, such as this, did nothing to enhance the group's musical side.

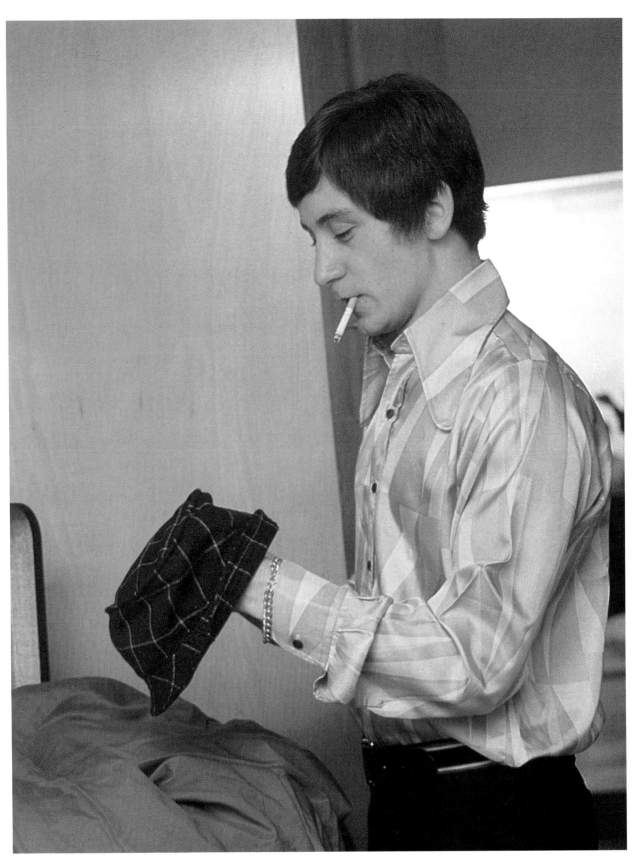

Kenney contemplates his wardrobe.

Classic snap circa 1966.

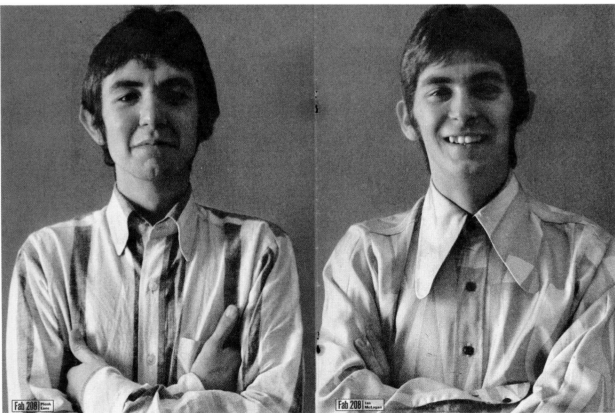

FAB 208's pin-ups from April 1967.

Ronnie Lane once worked in a clothes shop until he hit a salesman with a window pole.

STEVE MARRIOTT

Steve as a *Rave* centrefold.

Days of wine and song for Steve.

Dressing room smiles.

You may know a man by his shoes . . .

Marriott at work in his Chiswick pad.

The Small Faces perform for the camera.

Top: The Small Faces appear in *Jackie*, circa 1967. Bottom: The boys pose for *Record Mirror*, circa 1967.

SMALL FACES
TOP POPS

Top: Another 'Top of the Pops' kind of day. Bottom: Faces at a fairground.

The changing Faces. Top: 1966, young, sharp and handsome. Bottom: 1968, tired and bewildered.

Aged five, Mac wanted a pony, a kilt and a guitar.

go and play snooker,' says McLagan, whose subsequent frustration with the instrument persuaded him to move on to guitar. Some months later, he joined his school band, The Blue Men.

'The Blue Men were a skiffle group at that time,' McLagan recalled. 'We did Lonnie Donegan numbers like "Rock Island Line" and "Cumberland Gap".' The venture didn't last long.

After leaving school, McLagan enrolled at Twickenham Art School, and it was there that he switched back to keyboards and formed his own group, The Muleskinners. The primary reason behind the group's formation was that McLagan organised dances at the college, booking acts such as Cyril Davis or The Rolling Stones, whom he admired.

'I used to go and see The Stones every Sunday night at The Richmond Station Hotel,' he recalled, 'and I knew their booking agent, Eric Easton. One night I told him about the group I was in and he booked us on a tour with The Stones as the opening act. I was the singer at the time.'

Unfortunately, McLagan's art college was not

particularly impressed with their student's extra-curricular progress. After his first year he was threatened with expulsion unless he completed a heavy load of missed work over the summer holidays.

'So over the last few days of summer,' McLagan recalls, 'I did this work and was let back in for the second year. I got my grant, which in those days was about one hundred and twenty pounds. Then I used to get on the bus, miss the stop for the college, get off at the next stop and go to the pub and wait for all my friends to turn up. That was how I managed to spend my grant. So I wasn't able to continue.'

The Muleskinners actually signed to Fontana in late 1964 and released a single, 'Back Door Man'/'I Need Your Lovin'' in January of the following year. The record failed to chart.

That year, 1965, McLagan quit the band and in July joined Boz's People, a group put together by noted bassist Boz Burrel. The association was to last four months. Throughout this time, McLagan, who admired Boz's musical skill, found himself increasingly agitated by the bassist's easy-going ways.

'He wasn't bothered with doing anything,' McLagan recalls. 'He was really annoying me at the time because he was a great laugh but he was really lazy.'

A respite from the situation came when McLagan, whose skilful playing was now starting to gain attention, was invited to play on The Byrds's debut tour of Britain. Previously known as The Jet Set and The Beefeaters, before finally settling on The Byrds, Roger (later Jim before recently returning to Roger) McGuinn, Michael Clark, Chris Hillman and Gene Clark were an American group from Los Angeles heavily influenced by Britain's burgeoning Mod scene. In fact one of the reasons they cited for coming to Britain was to shop in Carnaby Street, the mecca of clothes for London's Modernists. The tour lasted for two and a half weeks in August 1965 and took McLagan all over the country. One of the most prestigious dates was an appearance on 6 August at the Flamingo Club in Soho, a legendary Mod club. McLagan himself was not a Mod but he could adapt quite easily, a trait that was to stand him in good stead the following year.

Mac in his auntie's garden.

After the Byrds tour, McLagan returned to Boz's People, but impatience and an increasing disillusionment with the set-up soon crept in. 'My wage packet,' he recalls, 'got smaller and smaller each week and I was sick of careering up and down the country humping my gear about.'

The inevitable occurred one Saturday when the group set out for a gig in Scotland. Somewhere near the Chiswick flyover, the van broke down. Boz's reaction to the situation was to break out laughing and McLagan realised that, as far as professionalism was concerned, he was simply wasting his time with this group. He got out of the van and walked away.

The following day he went over to his girlfriend's house in Manor Park and that night caught the last train back to Hounslow. Boarding the train he bumped into a friend named Phil, who asked him how his group was doing. McLagan told him of the previous day's events and how he had just quit the group. His friend informed him that a certain manager, called Don Arden, had been putting out feelers for an organ player. Mac should apply.

There is no way, thought McLagan, that I'm good enough to turn professional.

But he was wrong.

A youthful Ian McLagan.

"**O**KAY, everyone to their places," came the shout. "Stand by— ACTION!"

I watched, fascinated. Well, it's not every day that you get the chance to see scenes for a film being shot, and when those scenes include one of your favourite groups, it's even more exciting.

I was in Watford's Top Rank ballroom watching The Small Faces shoot a couple of scenes for their first film, a thriller called 'Deadline For Diamond.'

Although it's a thriller, the boys play themselves in the film, and in the scene I saw they had to drive up to the dance hall and then make a dramatic entrance, pushing their way through crowds of swarming fans.

After a few takes the Director said everything was okay and called a break for tea.

The boys asked me to join them, and we all went upstairs where the four young Londoners (who incidentally have only been together as a group for a few months) flopped down into armchairs to relax.

"Filming's a gas, but it's pretty tiring," said Steve Marriott, their eighteen-year-old vocalist and guitarist. "When we've finished tonight I'll just go straight home to bed."

Steve by the way, is no stranger to the cinema screen 'cos before he joined the group he was an actor and had appeared in four major films—one with Peter Sellers.

"Yea, Steve's right," agreed bass player Ronnie Laine (nicknamed PLONK), "we have a great time filming, but it certainly takes it out of you."

APPEARANCE-WISE, The Small Faces are very mod, but organist Jimmy Winston (he's the tallest of the four) hastened to tell me that this wasn't any kind of gimmick.

"No," said Jimmy, taking off his shades, "it's just that the clothes we like happen to be mod styles. We wear 'em 'cos we like 'em."

"I've been wearing this kind of jacket for ages," added drummer Kenny Jones, pointing to his coat of many colours. "I reckon it's good gear."

As the other boys were wearing similar clothes to Kenny I decided they were all going to be in agreement where gear was concerned.

Hobbies are out with The Small Faces at the moment—no time—but horse riding is the boys' favourite pastime—when there is time, though Jimmy is not too sure about this right now.

It so happened that while he was riding just recently Jimmy decided to offer his horse a lump of sugar. The horse threw its head round so sharply that poor old Jim was caught off balance. Result—one contented horse, and one bruised pop-star.

Mind you, Jimmy doesn't exactly rely on horses for transport. He owns a hundred m.p.h. Triumph T.R.4,

There's nothing ICKYBOO about the

Small FACES

says DOUG PERRY who reports on them for FAB

which gets him around rather more quickly. Plonk told me that he hopes to get a similar car soon.

ON their occasional days off, the boys enjoy going to the cinema, but their filmic tastes vary. Steve likes Peter O'Toole, Kenny goes for Anita Ekberg, while Jimmy raves over Marlon Brando.

Having been together for such a short time The Small Faces haven't yet found the chance to work abroad, but Steve told me how keen they were to go to the States.

"I'd like to visit America just out of curiosity," he said. "You hear so much about the place that you sort of can't wait to see it. Also I might get the chance to see some of my favourite artists over there. People like James Brown and Bobby Bland."

"I fancy going to Sweden," said Plonk. "Don't know why—I just fancy it."

Jimmy said he didn't really mind where they went, he'd just be content to see the world.

Even busy groups manage to have lots of fun and get into some comical situations, and The Small Faces are no exception. Not too long back they were staying at a hotel, and as Kenny didn't feel so well he decided to have an early night. So off he went for a nice peaceful "kip," while the other boys sat around chatting in the next room. About ten minutes later they heard a tremendous bang from Kenny's room, and they all rushed in to find Kenny trying to fight his way out of a great pile of sheets and blankets.

"Help!" yelled Kenny. "The bed's collapsed!" And between fits of laughter the boys managed to pull him out.

"**I** BET Kenny wasn't up very early the next morning," I said.

"The next morning," replied Kenny. "You're joking! It takes me all my time to get up ANY morning. I'm just hopeless first thing."

"Yeah, getting up's very ICKY-BOO," said Plonk.

"Beg your pardon," I said.

"ICKYBOO," he repeated. "It's a word we use for anything we don't like. We say it's ICKYBOO!"

I struggled to spell the word, and finally gave my note-pad and pen to Plonk, who wrote it in enormous-sized letters across the page.

"It would have been a lot easier to say that we just hate getting up," laughed Steve.

Just then their road manager came along to say that the boys were needed again on the film set, and the four of them strolled off happily to work.

About half-an-hour later they were back, and Steve, flopping down into his armchair, said that they'd finished for the day.

"How did that scene go," I asked.

"Pretty well," said Steve. "But, you know, filming's not ICKY-BOO—it's great."

Article covering the film *Dateline Diamond* in which The Small Faces appeared in 1965.

A pop pic book cashing in on the band's first hit.

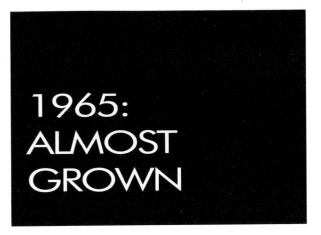

1965: ALMOST GROWN

After a few weeks of rehearsals, Marriott, Lane, Jones and Winston felt confident enough to throw in their jobs and turn semi-professional. It wasn't much of a decision – all had dead-end work which bored and depressed them. Kenney Jones, for example, after leaving school at fifteen, had taken a job bottling pickles at the Speciality Foods factory in Stepney. It was mind-numbing and after a month he told Ronnie Lane that he needed a change. Lane found him a job at his workplace, Selmer's in Chancery Lane, Holborn. Jones' task was to make up the amplifiers which were then passed on to Lane for testing.

'But he would always send mine back,' Jones ruefully recalls, 'even though I made the best ones.'

Lane worked out of his own soundproofed room and he and Jones knocked out a hole in the wall to create a personal restroom. Using a huge amplifier

to hide the entrance, they would crawl into this space to hold card games and illegal smoking sessions right under the nose of their foreman.

'There was a Polish guy there called Felix,' Jones remembers, 'who would see me go into Ronnie's room and not come out. So he would rush in and, of course, I wasn't to be seen. Ronnie told me he even used to look under cushions trying to figure out where I was. The hole we had built led on to the assembly line so I would just nip back there. Felix would come out of Ronnie's office and see me working away on the assembly line as if nothing had happened.'

When he wasn't gambling or smoking, Lane displayed his artistic talents by covering the walls of his room with cartoon characters. These were either original creations, such as Albert Frigg, or caricatures of famous people. (His co-workers apparently preserved the majority of these pictures but they have never surfaced.)

A regular visitor at Selmer's was Steve Marriott, and, true to form, mischief was not far behind. The real purpose of Marriott's visits, apart from hanging out with his friends, was to secure a free PA for the band. To that end, he had enlisted Jones and Lane's help. Which is why, no doubt after a session in 'the house', the management were treated to Lane testing the designated PA with the words, 'Free PA for Marriott, testing-testing-testing. Free PA for Marriott.'

Incidents such as these, along with Lane and Jones' inability to arrive at work on time, ensured that the duo were eventually handed their cards and sent packing. Lane and Marriott then took jobs washing dishes at the Lyon's Corner House in Stepney. They lasted one day.

'My mother and father kept on at me to get a decent job but playing in groups is all I wanted to do. So I played it shrewd. I got a job at Lyon's Corner House, washing up, and a few weeks later I dropped a crate with about three thousand dishes in it. It was an accident. But it was one of those dead-end jobs you get out of in a hurry and when they gave me the boot I was the happiest bloke alive. I tell you, a couple of weeks and I was playing with a group again. Great. And me mum and dad couldn't say much. I did try an ordinary job, didn't I?'

STEVE MARRIOTT, FEBRUARY 1965

'I'll always remember it,' says Jones, 'because on their first day there I went to meet them after work. I was standing by the bus stop and I had on these green shoes which I was really proud of and couldn't stop looking at. Steve and Ronnie came out and they had already been fired.'

Lane then landed another job, this time as messenger boy for the appropriately titled Ministry of Defence (MOD). Once again, it was a short-lived appointment. One lunchtime he had met up with Marriott and Jones at the Giaconda café in Denmark Street, their West End hang-out. Lane had a folder with him which the boys decided to open. Inside were top-secret plans for a nuclear submarine. Within minutes, they had managed to place the country's security at risk by spilling meat pie, brown sauce and coffee all over the designs. Not surprisingly, Lane was given his marching orders.

Shortly afterwards, the group reconvened at the Giaconda. 'I remember,' Jones says, 'we sat down and went, that's it, we're packing in the jobs. We're going to turn semi-professional.'

According to Marriott, though, the band were still on the look out for a guitarist. 'You've got to realise,' he stressed to me, 'that we formed out of error . . . We couldn't get anyone to join the group. The name [which had now become The Small Faces] put them off. I remember sitting in the Giaconda and trying to tout for guitarists. They'd

say, "What's the name of the group?" because in those days it was a very heavy thing. I'd say, whispering, "The Small Faces," and they'd go, "Fuck off, you've got to be joking." It embarrassed them, so in the end I thought, fuck it, I'll play guitar. I knew my way around it but I wasn't proficient at it.'

'Success,' Jones says, 'never once entered our heads. We didn't even think about it.' It was in this spirit (a spirit which the band desperately tried to hold on to throughout their careers) that the group packed their equipment into a van and hit the road. They had no dates booked or any engagements to fulfil but that didn't deter them.

Their set list consisted of R & B standards, such as James Brown's 'Please Please Please', Smokey Robinson's 'You Really Got A Hold On Me' and Ben E. King's 'Stand By Me', plus two original songs: 'Come On Children' and 'E Too D'. And thanks to Anabelle, a friend of Marriott's, they had the name. The Small Faces.

'The term "Face" was a top Mod, a face about town, a respected chap!' explained Marriott. 'The name came from a girl called Anabelle I knew from Chelsea. I didn't know many from Chelsea but I knew this one! Anyway, she signed the hire purchase agreement for my amplifier. We were trying to think of a name and she said, "Call yourselves The Small Faces," coz she said we were all little and had little boat races. It was great for us because it fitted in with us wanting to be Faces anyway.'

'Except Jimmy,' explains Kenney Jones, 'who was too tall.'

Though his height may have been a minor problem, it was through Jimmy that the group had transport, thanks to the availability of his brother Frank's van. (The group actually made a contract with Frank, signing a piece of paper that stated if they ever made any money, he would receive a percentage. Eight years later, Frank unsuccessfully attempted to take the group to court for breaking this 'contract'.)

'We just got in the van,' says Kenney Jones, 'and thought, "Right, let's go on the road." We had no idea where we were going but knew that's what you did in a band, just go up North and play. We had no bookings or nothing. We broke down in

Knutsford and we had to sleep in the van in a garage while Jimmy got the train back to London to get another one. Anyway, we all fall asleep in the van and Ronnie gets up to go for a piss. It's pitch black and he's fumbling around outside. Next thing I know there was this funny noise. So we all get out of the van and go looking for Ronnie. We're all shouting, "Ronnie Ronnie," until someone saw him. He had fallen down the engineer's pit and was lying there upside-down.'

The next day the band awoke starving and broke. Between them they had just three pence. Jones volunteered to try to buy some food and walked twelve miles to the nearest village.

'When I got there, there was only a baker's shop which had a cake for four pence. I had to get the guy to let me off a penny and then I walked all the way back to the van and we scoffed the cake. Great days.'

To secure work, Marriott had brought along an agent friend of his, Terry (later to be named Amphibious Egg) to cajole club owners into letting them play at their venues. His first success was at a tough working men's club in Sheffield where he managed to convince the owner that the band not only had their own material but were also more than capable of playing the covers and golden oldies that audiences would demand. This gig would turn out to be a very bitter-sweet experience for the travelling Mod minstrels.

When The Small Faces walked on stage that night, they must have wondered what they had let themselves in for. The crowd was made up of ageing Teddy Boys and hard-drinking workers, an audience not renowned for its tolerance of 'soft' Southerners dressed in neat clothes. What's more, the crowd had expected a cabaret band playing the oldies.

Needless to say, halfway through the set, just as they were about to launch into 'Please Please Please', the owner pulled the plugs. Annoyed and dispirited, the group left the club and wandered aimlessly around the Sheffield streets.

'We were paid off after three numbers,' Marriott recalled. 'We walked through the streets feeling utterly brought down. Then we came to the entrance

'We went on stage and started the act we'd planned. Halfway through the manager stopped us, said he was sorry but we were just not right for a working men's club. Anyway he paid us before we left. But strangely enough there was a woman of about sixty who loved us. She knew all the James Brown numbers we played and kept asking for more. The other people, however, just didn't go for our kind of music.'

STEVE MARRIOTT ON THE SMALL FACES'S DEBUT GIG
IN SHEFFIELD, OCTOBER 1965

of a club [The Mojo, then owned by a young Peter Stringfellow] that looked bright and with it. We could see lots of young people going in.

'On the spur of the moment, we went in and told the owner we would play for nothing. He agreed. We played for all we were worth, taking courage from the fact that the audience were mainly teenagers. All Mods in fact. Well, we went a bomb. The audience raved like mad and kept yelling for more. Although we told the owner we didn't want anything, he gave us a fiver each towards our expenses, so we went back to London happy. Or at least we started happy. What took the edge off things was that we ran out of petrol on the way back and had to wait for the filling station to open!'

Their next gig was in the relatively safe surroundings of the Ruskin Arms. Jimmy's mother had arranged the show and in the audience that night was the agent who worked for the Leicester Square Cavern Club. After seeing The Small Faces in action, he had no hesitation in rushing backstage and offering them a one-off Saturday night gig at his club.

It was an important breakthrough for the group. Not only was it their first West End gig but, thanks to the group's Mod image and chaotic energy, they filled the club out on the first night and created a scene for themselves. The engagement was extended to four more Saturday night shows and would take the group further than they had ever expected.

'Ronnie drew a picture of a Mod in a parka,' Marriott recalled, 'with The Small Faces painted on the back, like it was on Kenney's drum kit, which Ronnie had also painted. We put it outside the gig and it brought all these Mods in. We got the following straightaway down at the Cavern because we were Mods ourselves. It was a very cultish thing. At the time The Who were playing down the road at the Marquee. They were a bit Moddy too but I hadn't studied them and they hadn't heard of us.'

'There are many places in the North and Midlands that are as Mod – if not Moddier – than London. A crowd of rockers arrived at one of our gigs and we thought a punch-up likely. But they just formed themselves into a circle and danced about. It was great!'

STEVE MARRIOTT, OCTOBER 1965

Lane would later describe these early performances as, 'a chaotic lesson in bullshitting an audience. Fuck, we had some front! We used to take about an hour and a half to play four numbers. Steve had my Gretsch off me and he only knew about three chords and I'd only just bought this bass and we used to bullshit our way through. But he had such a lot of front, Steve did, that we got away with it.'

'We had six numbers,' Marriott said, 'and we played two hours with that. And then this Irishman would come up and say, "Can you play another two hours?" We'd say, "Yeah!" and repeat the whole thing. But we actually did have a following and we built this little thing up. We couldn't believe it ourselves. A following? We were packing the place out.'

Authenticity is crucial to the Mod lifestyle. Attention to detail paramount. The Small Faces were instantly welcomed by the capital's Modernists because they were Mods who had formed a band – they were not a band, like The Who, who had adapted to the image. This was a crucial difference.

'We admire The Who but we have never tried to copy them in any way. We are Mods and appeal to Mods but that's about all we have in common with them.'

RONNIE LANE, OCTOBER 1965

'It's very easy to say,' Marriott pointed out, 'that The Small Faces were the leaders of it but we weren't. We came to the top of the pile but at the same time we were just part of the movement. We weren't no spearhead.'

One of London's top 'faces' at the time was Pete Meaden who, along with Kit Lambert, co-managed The Who. It was Meaden who, in the words of author Richard Barnes, 'was in the process of masterminding the group into a Mod group,' and it was Lambert who, having heard about The Small Faces's spirited act and authentic Mod following, went down to the Cavern to check them out.

Although The Small Faces were a direct threat to The Who, Lambert instantly recognised their potential. He offered them a management deal, but his offer came too late. A man by the name of Pat Meehan Snr had beaten him to the punch.

Meehan worked for Contemporary Music, which also doubled as a management and production company. It had been started up by one of pop music's most legendary and flamboyant characters, Don Arden.

A former stand-up comic, singer and Master of Ceremonies, in 1959 Arden had compered Gene Vincent's UK tour. When the rocker moved to England, Arden agreed to manage him. It was an unhappy mix. The manager's famed aggression, coupled with the ageing singer's increasing alcohol problems, did not make for a smooth ride. In 1965, amid much acrimony, both parties went their separate ways.

Vincent's departure was not the only problem for the tempestuous Arden. While managing Vincent, he had made a killing promoting rock 'n' roll tours featuring American stars. The huge success of The Beatles had put pay to that. The Fab Four were not only a social phenomenon but a musical one as well. For the first time, UK audiences witnessed a British band that wrote and performed their own material. The response was overwhelming and the demand for the star US rock 'n' rollers, such as Jerry Lee Lewis and Little Richard, faded accordingly.

Arden noticed this change when a ten-week tour featuring American artists badly bombed, costing him a small fortune. He promptly dropped his rock 'n' roll connections and began searching for young UK-based pop groups.

Bowling over . . . Marriott at the Streatham Alley, 1965.

He found The Animals and then The Nashville Teens. Both partnerships were to end unhappily. In the case of The Teens, one particular incident fully explained why Arden had been dubbed the Al Capone of pop by his industry colleagues: Teens pianist John Hawken once made an impromptu visit to Arden's office to pick up some money. When he was handed a cheque that was one hundred pounds short, Hawken vociferously complained. Arden's response was to grab the hapless musician by the throat, drag him over to the window and threaten to push him out. Violent incidents such as these would dog Arden throughout his career.

When Meehan came back to Contemporary raving about The Small Faces, Arden agreed to go see them play.

The group themselves were not particularly fussed about who managed them. As Marriott once explained, 'We thought, we'll go with whoever offers the most dough.' (Marriott actually had a tenuous connection with Arden. The brusque manager's son, David, had been at acting school with him.)

The gig that Arden saw was memorable for two reasons: first, the manager was impressed by the group and immediately invited them to his office in Carnaby Street, which was situated above John Stephen's famous clothes shop. Second, both Marriott and Lane had gone on stage that night sporting severe cuts and bruises. Their injuries had been sustained the night before when they had caught the last train back from the West End to Loughton where Marriott was living, spending a lot of his time smoking dope and listening to Jimmy McGriff records.

As they were walking home, a van had pulled up and a bunch of men had piled out and viciously attacked them for no apparent reason. It was only later that Marriott and Lane discovered the motive behind the assault – revenge.

'It was a bunch of Tottenham boys,' Marriott explained. 'Apparently Woodford and Loughton had done up a bit of Tottenham. They all bundled out of this van as me and Ronnie were walking home and gave us one of the severest kickings I've had. Me, like a tosser, said, "What's it all about?" and they come back and give me another kicking. The next day we played down the Cavern Club and every

time Ronnie hit a note his head would bleed, and my lip was out *here*, and my eyes were out *here*. We must have looked *fearsome*.'

If the group were worried that their battered appearance might put off prospective managers, they had nothing to fear. If anything, their wounds were a plus in Arden's eyes and he warmed to their street attitude and charm. He even went as far as phoning Marriott's mother to convince her, and by proxy her son, of the benefits of signing with him. On 10 June 1965, The Small Faces signed with Arden's Contemporary Music.

Kenney Jones recalls, 'Don said, "Now listen, you can have a straight wage or a percentage deal." So we went outside in a huddle and said, "We ain't stupid, we want a wage *and* a percentage." We went back in and told him and he agreed to give us twenty pounds a week, plus a percentage of the records and a shopping account in every clothes shop in Carnaby Street.'

For the young, naive but clothes-conscious boys, such an offer was irresistible. Twenty pounds a week was a decent wage in the mid-sixties and the offer of free clothing to the four Mods was an extremely shrewd move by Arden. The group reacted accordingly. The following year, it was calculated that they spent some twelve thousand pounds on clothes. 'We were like old women at a jumble sale,' says Lane. 'Half the stuff we got we never even wore. We'd get home and think, "What did I buy that for?"'

'Any money we got,' Marriott explained, 'or money we could hold on to, went on clothes. There used to be a little knot of us from the East End and we would go down to Carnaby Street, which is nothing like it is now, of course. It was a very dowdy little street with very gloomy little shops. They were very small shops but very exclusive. They were also expensive but very stylish.'

Having signed to Contemporary, things seemed to move at breakneck speed. Arden's first task was to commission Ian Samwell to write the group's debut single. Samwell was a well-known songwriter, having penned 'Move It', which Cliff Richard took into the top ten in 1959. Perceived as the first ever British rock 'n' roll song, Samwell was revered in pop circles.

1965 Gered Mankowitz shot. Winston's height would prove to be his undoing.

He and his partner, Brian Potter, didn't let their new clients down, presenting them with a tune called 'What'cha Gonna Do About It'.

'We had a couple of meetings with Ian Samwell,' Kenney Jones recalls. 'He lived in Hampstead then. We went into IBC studios with him, and Glyn Johns was the engineer. We recorded "What'cha" and the B-side which Jimmy Winston sang on and played on with his homemade Lesley guitar.'

Though the riff was a blatant steal from Solomon Burke's 'Everybody Needs Somebody To Love', of which The Rolling Stones had recently recorded a version for their second album, the band were totally behind the song.

'We loved "What'cha Gonna Do About It",' Marriott said. 'It was a total nick of "Everybody", but so what? It didn't matter, it was a good record just the same.' The song's title had been lifted from Doris Troy's Atlantic single, which was a Mod favourite of the time.

The engineer on the session, Glyn Johns, would work with The Small Faces throughout their career. He would also later work with The Beatles, The Who and The Rolling Stones, among many others, and establish himself as one of the 'name' producers of his time. Surprisingly, his entry into studio work had come about in a very diffident way.

'I had no knowledge in recording, or interest in it,' he says. 'I was very interested in music. I was in a band, tinkered around like most teenagers. Somebody knew somebody who knew somebody who managed a recording studio, IBC studios in Portland Place, and I got an interview and that was it.

'I knew Ian Samwell and I remember him coming in with the band and I thought they were great. I thought they were an interesting bunch of guys because of their size and the energy that came out of them.'

While the group worked on Samwell and Potter's offering, Arden was busy securing a distribution deal through Decca. With that achieved, The Small Faces's debut single, 'What'cha Gonna Do About It'/'What's A Matter Baby' (written by Otis Byers) was released on 6 August 1965. The B-side had already been recorded by singer Timi Yuro, in straightforward pop fashion, but in The Small

Faces's hands the song was shorn of its lightweight pop trappings and given an energetic infusion of R & B. It was all part of the group's plan to bring the music they loved to a mass audience.

'We used to do a cover,' Marriott said, 'and then say, fuck that, listen to the original, it's much better.'

Such subtleties, however, were lost on Decca who put very little promotion behind the record bar mentioning it in their weekly NME advert, along with the rest of their releases. This attitude, according to Johns, was the prevalent one among major companies such as Decca, who had no real understanding of either pop music or its audience.

'The record business in England was incredibly backward compared to the United States,' Johns points out. 'Rock 'n' roll had started in America and had been going for some time and it was very difficult for rock 'n' roll to get established because it was Black man's music. Most of the people in charge over here had absolutely no idea what made it work or why it worked. They didn't understand it.

'Aside from people like Billy Fury, who was copying the Americans anyway, there hadn't been a similar movement. The Small Faces, The Who and various other bands came along, all copying what they were hearing from across the Atlantic but with a different twist to it. The fashion thing, the hair, the clothes, the whole Mod thing. Nobody at the record company got that. They didn't understand that side of it. By the time the first Small Faces LP was done that was in the past because they had woken up to the fact that there was an enormous amount of money to be made out of this stuff.'

A month later 'What'cha Gonna Do About It' entered the charts at twenty-seven. Three days after that, The Small Faces dominated Friday night TV, appearing on BBC1's Crackerjack at 5 p.m. and an hour later on Rediffusion's legendary pop show Ready Steady Go.

Many people attributed the single's success, as it swiftly rose to number fourteen, to the TV appearances. But there was another reason for the record's meteoric rise in the charts: chart fixing. In Johnny Rogan's Starmakers and Svengalis, a history of British pop management, the author quotes Arden on the subject:

Early Decca promo shot.

The Small Faces's original line-up makes its debut on *Ready Steady Go* performing 'What'cha'.

'I knew that for certain sums, any record I was associated with could be elevated to the charts,' Arden reveals. 'It got to be a habit. I paid out anything from one hundred and fifty pounds to five hundred pounds a week to people who manipulated the charts and who in turn shared the cash with people organising other charts so as to ensure they tallied . . . Neat little swindle, wasn't it? Of course The Small Faces had no idea what went on.'

That the group were kept in the dark from these behind-the-scenes machinations is no surprise. Not only were they totally innocent of the business they had just entered, but it was doubtful whether they even had the time to sit down and think about such things. They were working far too hard for such luxuries, for Arden applied the same strategy to them as he did to all his groups – put them out on the road to play an endless string of one-nighters all over the country.

Conscious of the 'here today, gone tomorrow' nature of many pop acts, managers often took a short-term view where their artists were concerned,

milking them for as long as they could before their popularity faded. The Small Faces were no exception.

As the single climbed the charts, media and fan interest mushroomed. For The Small Faces, evidence of their fame came with their live gigs, where screaming girls would rush the stage and cut short the act. Often mini riots would take place, ensuring that the group were 'unofficially' banned from many venues. Such public adoration was a totally new experience and it took the group some time to put their fame into perspective.

'At first, it was great for your ego,' says Jones, 'and for about six months I had a big head, we all

'We've been besieged with "Gonks" toys and little furry thingamebobs from fans. Terry, our road manager, piled them up in our dressing room after each show. There were two practically life-size dolls of me and Plonk and we were thinking of sending them on stage instead of us so we could get some sleep.'

STEVE MARRIOTT, MAY 1966

'We've met quite a few well-known groups who have been playing for some years and they all warn us that after a while we won't think it's as much fun as it is just now. But we'll worry about that when the time comes.'

did for a while. But we did get fed up with it. To be honest, we tried to play as best we could live and ignore the screams. If that was happening out there, that was happening out there, we were just playing for us on stage. We really enjoyed playing with each other and sometimes the screams and the girls jumping on stage was a real drag. It's like someone throwing a brick while you're on stage.'

Ronnie Lane recalls, 'I coped all right, after all it was right up my street. It was exciting, man. There were chicks around and I was a pop star. But I tell you something, it was quite violent. They really wanted to get hold of you.'

Dazed by their unexpected success, there was only one problem looming and that was Jimmy Winston.

'Jimmy went off his rocker every now and then, plus we didn't get on too well personally,' Marriott explained. 'So it was decided by the three of us that Jimmy should go. It was due to a lot of little things. Like we did *Thank Your Lucky Stars* with "What'cha Gonna Do About It" and it came to that guitar part which I was proud of because it was my first solo on

record, and I'd go and do it and suddenly Jimmy would go apeshit in the corner, waving and jumping about so the cameras would be on him. So he had to go, which was hard because he had the van and he didn't want to go.'

Confirming Marriott's dislike of Winston, Lane says of the organist, 'He was a bighead and I don't think Steve could take it any more. He had no talent as such, but his father ran a pub which was kind of helpful in a way.'

Kenney Jones felt the same way. 'He was only learning and he was wholeheartedly into it, but he was useless and a complete distraction from Steve. All those guitar poses and he was taller. It just wasn't happening. So one day he turned up at a gig and he wasn't on it, we had got so fed up with it. We were a bit unkind to him because no one would talk to him and he couldn't understand why he wasn't in the group any more. He came along to the gig and we had a new organist.'

The show was a prestigious slot at the Lyceum and the new member was, of course, Ian McLagan. As fate would have it, Marriott had read a review of a Boz's People gig in *Melody Maker* which had singled McLagan out for praise. The accompanying photo was actually of Boz Burrell but the caption ran, 'McLagan's keyboard playing shone.' Marriott asked Arden to contact him.

The phone rang at McLagan's house the day after his train conversation with his friend Phil. It was

One of the first photo sessions with Mac.

Arden's secretary requesting McLagan come up to Carnaby Street the next day. Amazed by the co-incidence, McLagan dutifully presented himself at the office.

'When I got the call no one said what band it was I had to see. I was up there most of the day waiting and I was looking at the pictures Arden had on the wall of The Animals, The Nashville Teens, The Small Faces and this other group, The Claymen Squares,

he like, what's he like?" and Don's going, "He seems like a very nice lad," and we all go, "Yes, but how big is he?"

Steve Marriott always maintained that there was something magical about The Small Faces's formation. Which is why, when the tiny organist walked in to meet the group, Marriott reportedly hugged him on the spot.

'I couldn't believe,' Marriott recalled, 'that there

The East End's answer to The Beatles.

or something. Well, I knew The Animals and The Nashville Teens had keyboard players, The Small Faces would never really want someone like me, so I figured it was the Claymen group. And then, finally, Don Arden called me in and The Small Faces were standing there.'

'Don had got him up to the office,' Marriott recalled, 'and had him waiting outside in reception so we didn't see him. We were all asking, "What's

was a guy standing there in front of us who was already one of us. The vibes were perfect although he was shy at the time. His humour was perfect and all I could do was hug him because it was just like he'd been missing.'

All the group instinctively warmed to Ian McLagan, a feeling that Kenney Jones would later articulate:

'I was over the moon when Mac joined. I suddenly

'When I met the other Faces it was like looking at a mirror of myself – I couldn't believe it. We all looked alike – Plonk and Steve might have been my brothers. It was about the first time that I've ever counted myself lucky to be small because apart from needing a new organist, I fitted the group image of being little.'

IAN MCLAGAN ON JOINING THE GROUP,
SEPTEMBER 1966

had something to play with. I didn't realise until that point what I'd been missing out on until we got a proper keyboard player in. Suddenly, this big hole was filled up soundwise. I started playing a little differently, much better, and it was great. We all loved Mac.'

'It just happened that way. We're just mates who happened to hit it off. Somebody didn't say, right, let's get a little crowd of little blokes together and form a big group.'

STEVE MARRIOTT, FEBRUARY 1965

The addition of a new member threw up some practical problems. First, McLagan was not a Mod. He had little interest in the youth cult. Arden ordered him to get a haircut and gave him some money to buy the proper attire. And he also added that year to his birthdate.

More pressing was the imminent release of the group's next record. Buoyed by the success of their debut single, both band and manager had chosen a Marriott and Lane song, 'I Got Mine', coupled with 'It's Too Late'.

The A-side had already been recorded prior to McLagan's arrival and featured a guitar part by Jimmy Winston. To promote the single the group had agreed to appear at London's Lyceum for a Radio Luxembourg live show. McLagan, therefore, made his live debut with The Small Faces holding a guitar and miming to Winston's guitar pattern.

'That was a gas that record,' McLagan recalled. 'They had already recorded it with Jimmy so they took me down to a shop in Charing Cross Road and got me this guitar which I had to play. They wanted me to learn it but I never really did. But I mimed it for ages on Thank Your Lucky Stars and all those other television things.'

The day after McLagan's 'debut' the group travelled to Swindon. In the space of that day, McLagan learnt the set and that night made his proper debut with the group. Two days later, Bonfire Night 1965, 'I Got Mine' was released.

The main thrust of the single's promotion was planned around a film, Jeffrey Sumner's Dateline Diamonds (Rank) which the group (with Winston) had participated in earlier that year. The plotline revolved around a jewel theft and a pirate radio station, run by Kenny Everett, who at the time DJed at many of London's Mod clubs, such as Tiles. The film also featured Kiki Dee and The Chantells.

The Small Faces' biggest scenes occur at the end when they perform a short live set, including 'I Got Mine'. It was intended that both film and song would appear at the same time and promote each other, but editing delays meant that the single had long disappeared by the time the film was eventually released in April 1966.

For the single, Decca took out a special half-page advert in the NME featuring two photos of the band. The critics themselves raved about the record.

'The reviews for that single,' Marriott remembered, 'were incredible, five-star ratings saying The Small Faces are here to last, they've proved with this record how talented they are. I was so chuffed it didn't matter if it was a hit or miss because it hit home with the critics.'

Unfortunately, despite their increasing live work and TV appearances, the single nose-dived. A week after its release, the band appeared on Ready Steady Go alongside The Nashville Teens, Wilson Pickett, The Sorrows and Tom Jones. In November they played gigs in Colchester, Cleethorpes, Aylesbury, Swindon, Wimbledon, Stortford, Birmingham, Llannelly, Morecambe, Rawtenstall, Guildford and Herne Bay. Yet still the single refused to sell. It was their first taste of defeat in Arden's hands.

A brighter note came in December when, at the NME's Fourteenth Annual Popularity Poll, The Small Faces came sixth, with The Seekers, The Walker Brothers, The Yardbirds, The Who and The Fortunes placed above them.

It was a promising start for a band who had

November 1965 and Ian McLagan makes his *Ready Steady Go* debut.

formed just six months previously, but Don Arden was not a man to be impressed by statistics or critical acclaim. Sales were what mattered and at this crucial stage he wasn't about to risk another flop by issuing a second Marriott/Lane song. Instead he turned the job over to a professional songwriting duo, Kenny Lynch and Mort Shuman. They came back with 'Sha La La La Lee'.

'I admired Mort Shuman for the work he had done with Elvis Presley,' Marriott revealed. 'I was totally knocked out by the fact that he performed it for us sitting at the piano. I can't put the record down because we did our best with it. But what bugged me was Kenny Lynch. He wrote it and produced it and ended up bleedin' singing on it, doing backing vocals. That's him doing the high-pitched la la la la's. I know I've been a bit hard on him in the past but he was a fucking nuisance. He was a songwriter cum self-plugger. That's all he was there for, to sell his songs.'

According to Jones, it took the group four hours just to play the record's intro correctly, a sign of their nervousness regarding the song's quality. A bright if lightweight pop tune, it wouldn't be released until the following year and would seriously damage the band's ambitions to be the UK's answer to soul acts such as Booker T and the MGs.

As their gig schedule increased it was decided among the group that it would be practical to live together. There was only one dissenter, Kenney Jones, who opted to stay on at his parents' house in Stepney, although for press purposes this was never revealed.

'I couldn't stand the late nights,' Jones explained. 'I'm a morning person, always have been so. The press at the time made this thing out of the fact that we all lived together, so I would get to Pimlico in the mornings in time to join in whatever was happening. Usually it was nothing and a complete waste of time because none of the others would get up until four or sometimes six in the evening.'

On Boxing Day 1965, the group (minus Jones who was given a room none the less) moved into 22 Westmoreland Terrace, Pimlico, a beautiful Georgian house situated in an exclusive area near Victoria. Their new living quarters had been supplied by Arden but were paid for out of the band's money.

'It's great. See, the thing is it's so convenient being together all the time 'cause we can discuss our act and try new things out on the spur of the moment, not have to wait and arrange a rehearsal.'

STEVE MARRIOTT ON THE SMALL FACES' PIMLICO FLAT, SUMMER 1966

'Don got us that house,' Marriott remembered. 'It came with this old German woman, Liezel, who was mad. She did everything. Cooked, cleaned, sewed. She's still about. Everyone else saw how good she was and she started cleaning all these other rock 'n' roller's houses. She was cool about things, cool with the gear, didn't say a word. For us she was like a nanny, she did the lot.'

In the following months the address would be besieged by fans anxious to meet their idols. At the end of the road, they covered a wall with graffiti messages of undying love (and caused such a fuss that the group were finally forced to find new

'Sometimes it's annoying but you get used to it [fans outside the house]. It's worse during the holidays. One girl just stood out there all day crying! Nobody had done anything to her. I suppose it was just her way of saying she likes us.'

STEVE MARRIOTT, SEPTEMBER 1966

homes). Their new pad would also attract some famous visitors.

'The house,' Marriott recalled, 'was always full of mentals like Marianne Faithfull, screaming and jumping about. I used to have to lock myself in the toilet and write songs in there.'

The Beatles' manager, Brian Epstein, also paid a visit but apparently only socially, business was never mentioned.

'There was a mutual friend of ours who knew Epstein,' McLagan recalls, 'and because Epstein was gay I think he wanted to meet these four young lads. Anyway, this friend brought him over and then spiked our drinks with LSD. We all started going a bit mad and Epstein, who hadn't had anything, couldn't handle it and went running out of the house. That was the first time we did LSD.'

1965 ended with a hectic, whirlwind Small Faces tour of Europe, the group travelling to Belgium, Holland, Denmark and Germany in the space of just six days. If this was a punishing schedule, it was only a taster of what 1966 had in store.

The Small Faces move into Pimlico. Liezel is there to play mum. Literally.

The Small Faces, circa 1966.

1966: BECOME LIKE YOU

Despite the failure of 'I Got Mine', The Small Faces were swiftly becoming the new pin-ups of the British pop scene. Adored by those whose elder brothers and sisters had taken to The Beatles or The Rolling Stones, their audience was young, excitable and, at live performances, often hysterical.

The group had barely reached their twenties and, combined with their youthful good looks and sharp sense of dress, were perfect teeny-bop material. Yet the adulation irked them. Young and handsome they may have been, but they primarily saw themselves as serious musicians, and uncritical mass adoration from sobbing, screaming teenagers was not what they sought.

A month after moving into their Pimlico residence, 'Sha La La La Lee'/'Grow Your Own' was released. Commercially, the single put the band right back on track.

'We became pop stars,' Marriott once noted, 'which we never really wanted to be. Not if you had integrity at all and smoked a little hash. To see all these young girls getting hurt in a crush and not being able to hear ourselves sing or play, we just wanted to go home.'

Ronnie Lane confirmed this sentiment. He likened the gigs to playing in a pub where everyone was talking and no one was listening. For the next two years, he asserted, the group didn't hear a single note they played on stage.

'You go out there and there's the kids pulling your shirt and your shoelaces, it's no good. How can you do an act? What can you do but just grin?'

RONNIE LANE, DECEMBER 1966

'And when they stopped screaming,' Lane says, 'and we could hear ourselves play, we weren't that good.'

Relatively speaking, these were still the early years of pop's development and, among other things, one of its main attractions was the ability to provide a public outlet for pre-pubescent emotions. All the major groups of this time had experienced the same phenomenon. In fact, it was one of the primary reasons behind The Beatles' decision, in 1966, to quit live work. Faced with halls filled with mass hysteria, each note the Fab Four played was lost in a whirlpool of screams – they could have been miming for all anyone cared. The same applied to The Small Faces.

What's more, the fans' wild reactions obscured

'Quite honestly I couldn't care if we were dropped by the kids and died as a group tomorrow. As long as we carried on making good records – that's all I care about.'

STEVE MARRIOTT, MAY 1967

The Small Faces perform on the steps of the Royal Albert Hall, circa 1966.

the creativity of artists who were genuinely concerned with producing music that was highly individual.

'When we started I used to love personal appearances but now I would rather be in the studio. As far as recording is concerned the sky's the limit.'

STEVE MARRIOTT, DECEMBER 1966

'Sha La La La Lee' was released midway through the band's first major UK tour. Two days before, the group had appeared on Granada's Wednesday night *Scene* show and in the same week they were given top billing in Decca's weekly *NME* advert.

After two weeks, the single entered the chart at number twenty. A month later it had climbed to number three, their first top-ten hit. But despite its success, the band were not particularly thrilled.

'I thought "Sha La La La Lee" was a bit of an iffy number,' Kenney Jones recalls. 'It was very commercial and slightly different from what was happening at the time, which was a lot of pretty little songs being sung with pretty little voices. It was a pretty song but sung with Steve's rough, powerful

'I'm not a singer. Singers sing. I go on stage and I just rave around. That's how we make our records. I sit down and work on a lyric while Plonk raves around me, keeping me awake. Tony Bennett sings, I don't. Mick Jagger raves. John Lennon sings. Scott Walker sings; he's probably the best singer on the scene at the present time. Singers are people like Frank Sinatra, whom I don't dig – but I dig his daughter!'

STEVE MARRIOTT, MAY 1966

Unusually stylish Decca photo, circa 1966.

voice. It was Don Arden's thing really. He said we couldn't afford another flop so we went with Kenny Lynch and, to be fair, he gave us a hit and it worked.'

Ronnie Lane had his misgivings also: '"Sha La La La Lee" was a good Saturday night dance record, but it wasn't what we were really good at, which was playing Black R & B. I think the rot began to set in around that time.'

'The group and I are utterly fed up with being regarded as childish little boys. We want to be regarded as mature people of sound mentality. But instead people continue to treat us as kids.'

STEVE MARRIOTT, MAY 1966

New band member, Ian McLagan, also had misgivings but they were not to do with the record. His doubts centred around money. 'Our live gigs,' Marriott recalled, 'were our livelihood. Regardless of what the band earned from the gigs, though, we were still on twenty pounds a week. When Mac joined he was on thirty pounds a week for six weeks and he created God knows how much fuss because he wanted to have the same as the band. So his money went down to twenty pounds a week! That's exactly what happened. He couldn't believe it. He was saying, "I don't want to be on a wage, I want to

Plonk and Mac pose for a fan.

feel part of the group." "Fine. Twenty pounds a week." He was dumbstruck.'

With 'Sha La La La Lee' riding high in the charts, the band's profile rose accordingly. The music papers, female teenage magazines, such as *Valentine*, through to the national press, all featured

'It alters your whole life and way of looking at things. The worst part is when you start believing the glowing reports about yourself in the papers. I went through a stage like that when "Sha La La La Lee" was number one. I soon got over it but even now I feel ashamed to think that I ever thought I was someone special.'

STEVE MARRIOTT, MARCH 1967

the group. And the gigs piled up as the band, night after night, walked on stage, played a few numbers to a screaming audience and then fought their way back to the van where they would smoke dope and try to forget what had just occurred.

'Whenever I see my old friends they always make cracks about me being big-headed. I don't think I am. I'm sure I haven't changed. It's their attitude towards me that has and it makes me feel very embarrassed when we meet.'

KENNY JONES, MARCH 1967

With The Beatles and The Rolling Stones winding down their performing schedules, The Small Faces were fast becoming the country's number one live attraction. But the unrelenting work schedule, the constant gigging and TV appearances were bound to exact a price.

On one occasion, McLagan remembered Ronnie Lane starting to talk nonsense. When he asked him what he meant, Lane replied that he had no idea, but as he was going mad it didn't matter!

In February, the band started a live stretch that would last four months. This included a lightning trip to Paris and a telerecording of inserts for their American TV debut on the *Dick Clark Show*. They also found time to appear in a Canadian TV documentary, filmed at London's Marquee club, in which the four Mods gave their views on the impending British general election.

In March, under orders from Arden, they pulled out of a gig with The Walker Brothers because of a dispute over billing, but in April they broke the attendance record (formerly held by Georgie Fame) at the Streatham Ice Rink.

'We'd been opening everything including *Five O'Clock Club*. They were beginning to call us The Small Openers. I mean, own up – we had a number in the top ten so let us be second or something.'

RONNIE LANE, SUMMER 1966

That month, a promoter also promised the group headline status, along with The Kinks, at a concert to be held at Edgware Town football ground. After another dispute, The Kinks this time pulled out, refusing to support The Small Faces.

In May, the group appeared alongside The Beatles and The Rolling Stones at the then prestigious *NME* Poll Winners' Concert at Wembley. Five days later, their fourth single 'Hey Girl'/'Almost Grown' was released.

In strict contrast to their preceding hit, 'Hey Girl' was a Marriott/Lane composition. 'It was a turning point,' Marriott said. 'Don allowed us to continue writing our own material and we knew we could deliver. Both me and Ron knew as soon as we heard "Sha La La La Lee" that it was a hit and in those days hit singles mattered, so "Hey Girl" was an extension of that. It was very "single" minded. We weren't worried about albums. In those days,

'I'm not sure when we wrote "Hey Girl" but it was before the leaves were on the trees and it was something to do with my mother's birthday.'

STEVE MARRIOTT, MAY 1966

Plonk and Mac: same smile, same height, same haircut, circa 1966.

Facing Facts

Born Kenneth Jones on 16th September, 1948, at Stepney, East London. Educated at St. George's In The East (!) and Stepney Green senior schools.

Height: 5 ft. 4 in.

Hair: Fair, and flatter than the other Faces . . . very neat. Has "a nice little hat, like a jockey cap with a shorter flap."

Eyes: Pale blue and rather beautiful.

Ties: Wears black knitted ties, with diamond-shaped tie-pin.

Chest: 36 in. Has stopped wearing sweaters, and is smartly turned out by Lord John's.

The drummer boy . . . used to put musical instruments together . . . tends to drum everything, at the most inopportune moments . . . the quiet Face who doesn't expect to be noticed and always is . . . likes un-quiet sports like riding horses and archery . . . doesn't drink pubbery drinks . . . has a horror of public transport . . . devoted to his mother and stays home to look after her . . . goes on about James Brown and The Hollies . . . the most sensitive Face.

Waist: 28 in.

Hips: 36 in.

Cufflinks: Occasionally wears cufflinks; prefers his triangular ones with the diamond in the middle.

Wrists: Wears impressive watch with white strap, bought by his mother for his 17th birthday. Occasionally wears identity bracelet with a medallion featuring The Bridge of Sighs.

Hands: Onyx ring on little finger. Also wears a gold sovereign, dated 1909, in ring form.

Shoes: Size 5½, from Toppers of Carnaby Street.

Born Steve Marriott on 1st January, 1947, at Bow, where they ring those East End bells. Went to Sandringham Secondary Modern.

Height: 5 ft. 4 in. worth.

Hair: Brown. Steve never wears a hat because "it messes me Barnet up."

Eyes: Deep-set and hazel. Watchful.

Eyes: Wide, clear and a pussycat green.

Collar: 14 in. Shirts are hand made by Frank Foster. Likes mauve stripes.

Collar: 14 in. Shirts usually bought from Lord John's in Carnaby Street.

Ties: Hates them —but sometimes wears knitted ones.

Chest: 36 in. Often wears hand-made sweaters sent to him by fans. Has suits and jackets made by Duggie Millings.

Stevie shares a flat in Pimlico, London, with Ronnie and Ian . . . he plays guitar, drums, piano, organ and harmonica . . . was taught to play uke by his father—at twelve, he starred in West End production of *Oliver!* for eighteen months . . . studied acting at the Italia Conti School for four years . . . had his own group pre-Faces called Steve Marriott and The Moments . . . owns fifty sweaters . . . uses Cockney rhyming slang!

Born Ronald Lane on April Fool's Day, 1946, at Plaistow, East London. Last known attempts at education at Lister Technical College, Plaistow.

Height: All 5 ft. 5 in. of him.

Hair: Dark brown. Wears an old cavalry hat while looning around.

Eyes: Hazel and busy.

Ties: He has one, but he wears it quite a lot. It's black knitted . . . surprise, surprise.

Chest: 38 in. Expanded. Buys Carnaby Street gear.

Ties: Has three knitted ones— light brown, dark brown and black.

Plays bass guitar . . . started off playing in East End pubs . . . drinks Cokes . . . fascinated by weird electronic sounds . . . writes songs, and is trying to write a book . . . sends money home to his parents . . . marathon phone caller . . . used to test amplifiers at Selmers' factory and left behind cartoons all over the factory walls, which have been preserved by workers . . . shepherd's pie addict . . . raves about Booker T. and James Brown.

Chest: 36 in. Buys jackets from Duggie Millings, sweaters from Carnaby Street boutiques.

Hips: 36 in.

Waist: 28 in.

Cufflinks: Wears cufflinks when possible. Likes onyx, not too big or flashy.

Wrists: No watch. Wears inch-wide gold bracelet engraved with "Plonk" from fan . . . "not too expensive but a nice thought."

Waist: 24 in. "Small, isn't it!"

Hips: 36 in.

Trouserlegs: 27 in. Trousers from Duggie Millings or Carnaby Street.

Born Ian McLagan, on 12th May, 1946, at Hounslow, Middlesex. Educated at Spring Grove Grammar School, Hounslow.

Height: 5 ft. 5 in. The biggest Face.

Hair: Brown. "I look terrible in hats. Haven't a hat head."

Collar: 13¾ in. Shirts made by Frank Foster.

Plays electric organ . . . the newest face, but doesn't consider himself new . . . previously played with The Muleskinners, The Boz People . . . collects labels to stick on walls . . . has a thing about cobblestones—they hurt his Carnaby Street feet . . . traffic wardens are bane of his life . . . in charge of group gonk, Sigmund . . . digs Alan Price, Otis Redding, Georgie Fame and soul sounds.

IAN McLAGAN

Cufflinks: No cufflinks. Shirts always have buttons.

Waist: 24 in.

Hips: 36 in.

Trouserlegs: 28 in. Trousers come from various Carnaby Street-ers.

Wrists: Doesn't like cluttering up his wrists with anything. Consequently has to ask Stevie the time, and Stevie has to ask Plonk.

Hands: Doesn't own any rings, but would like to have a "nice" one . . . "a one-off, that no one else could copy."

Shoes: Size 6. Bought from the good old Carnaby Street traders.

WEIGHING OFF

Steve Marriott	Kenny Jones
Weight: 8 st.	*Weight:* 9 st. The heaviest Face.
Ronnie Lane	Ian Mclagan
Weight: 8 st. 8lb.	*Weight:* 8 st.

Wrists: Doesn't wear a watch. "I've had three and I always smash them. I rely on other people for the time."

Hands: Wears a silver ring bought in Belgium; never wears gold.

Cufflinks: Has a very unusual "mystery" ring, with a huge stone "with scaffolding round it" bought at Lord John's.

Shoes: Size 5, from Toppers in Carnaby Street. Has a pair of fantastic green leather ones.

Trouserlegs: 27 in. Trousers from Carnaby Street.

Trouserlegs: 27 in. Trousers from Lord John's.

Hands: Not a ring man.

Shoes: Size 6. From Carnaby Street people.

FAB 208 presents the facts for the group's huge audience.

A fan's signed photos of the boys at the Starlight Ballroom, Paddington, 1966.

albums were done in three days, as was the first one. We wrote about 90 per cent of that album without a thought for how commercial it was going to be. It was all singles, singles, singles.'

'Steve and Ronnie,' Jones recalls, 'were getting in a very commercial phase starting with "Hey Girl", which was a bit frustrating because we had all these big hit successful singles, practically overnight, that we had to play live. As we only played for about twenty minutes they were using up an entire set and this started to interfere with what we really wanted to play, which was more of the album-orientated stuff, and this was getting confined to rehearsals.

'It would really piss us off when we went to see bands we considered rock or blues bands – people like Georgie Fame, The Yardbirds and Zoot Money – because that was how we saw ourselves. Not a pop band which is what we were live.'

The single entered the charts at sixteen, their highest entry to date, before reaching number ten. Shortly afterwards, the group's eponymously titled debut album was released. As Marriott had claimed, it had taken three days to record and more than confirmed the band's massive popularity by climbing to the number three position, staying there for seven weeks. It was a double triumph.

'That was a very natural album,' Jones states. 'We weren't slick musicians but we were very inven-

tive and it comes across in the arrangements. It showed who we were listening to: Booker T and the MGs, obviously Sam Cooke, whose "Shake" we used to open all our early gigs with, James Brown, and, for me, Charlie Mingus. It's got a great feel to it and it's a shame that as we progressed and became better musicians, we lost the riskiness that was so evident on that album. We just didn't care. Like Steve said, it was just crash, bang, wallop – singles, singles, singles.'

The album included seven original numbers, three songs from Kenny Lynch and partners, the Samwell/Potter 'What'cha' and a cover of Sam Cooke's 'Shake'. Jimmy Winston receives a credit on three of the tracks, but is not mentioned in the sleeve notes, nor is he depicted on the cover.

The critical reaction to the album mirrored its commercial success, being hailed in various quarters as one of the year's most exciting releases. A cross between Booker T and the MGs and The Who, meeting in Motown's Detroit studios, it bowled over critics and public alike and confirmed the potential of the Marriott/Lane partnership.

Glyn Johns, who had engineered on most of the sessions, says, 'Marriott had more energy and he was more blinkered. He was determined to do what he wanted to do with his music. He may well have been influenced by Booker T but he took that, like a

Marriott with man's best friend, Pimlico, 1966.

little terrier, and hurled it around the room a few times. Ronnie was the same although they were very different characters.

'Marriott was a bolshy little bugger. I never really liked him very much. I got on all right with him but he was cocky. He was obviously very insecure and he had a huge ego but he wouldn't have been the artist he was without it. Ronnie was a lot less aggressive. He was a milder individual although he wasn't all bells and whistles. He had an unpleasant side to him but Ronnie and Kenney were the two I got close to. The only time I spent with Marriott was when I was working. I never hung out with him.'

A few years later, one of the LP's outstanding tracks, the Marriott/Lane 'You Need Loving', cropped up again to create rock history, albeit in a different format.

'"Whole Lotta Love" by Led Zeppelin was nicked

'At first everything was just fabulous but it didn't stay like that. The trouble was that as Steve became more popular he gradually became more sensitive. I couldn't understand why his personality and temperament had changed so drastically. I just couldn't see how one day he could be so nice and the next day so horrible.'

SALLY FOULGER, STEVE MARRIOTT'S
EX-GIRLFRIEND, 1966

off that album,' Marriott pointed out. 'Percy Plant was a big fan. He used to be at all The Small Faces gigs. We did a gig with The Yardbirds which he was at and Jimmy Page asked me what that number was we did. "'You Need Loving'," I said, "it's a Muddy Waters thing" which it really is, so they both knew it, and Percy used to come to the gigs whenever we played in Kidderminster or Stowbridge, where he came from. He was always saying he was going to get this group together. He was another nuisance. He kept coming into the dressing room, just another little Mod kid. We used to say, "That kid's here again." Anyway we used to play this number and it became a stock opener after that album. After we broke up they took it and revamped it. Good luck to them. It was only old Percy who'd had his eye on it. He sang it the same, phrased it the same, even the stops at the end were the same, they just put a different rhythm to it.'

He laughs. 'For years and years I would hear it come on the radio while driving in America, and I would think, "Go on, my son," until one day I thought, "Fucking hell, that's us, that is. The bastards!"'

Making the album also allowed the group the rare luxury of hearing themselves within a live context. The studio became an aural mirror for the group, a sanctuary into which no screaming fans were allowed.

'We don't get enough time to work things out. We only get two-hour sessions. We want to get in the studio and do things properly. We'd get left behind if we kept on with the same thing all the time. But we haven't got the time to write. If we had weeks off, we'd be OK.'

RONNIE LANE, AUTUMN 1966

'We were more excited about hearing ourselves back,' Jones recalls, 'hearing what we sounded like. The studio was a welcome relief. We could jam together and we were a band. When we went out on the road, we could only play for twenty minutes but in the studio we could jam and from that came songs.'

It was an experience which sowed the seeds for the group's later preference for studio work. Yet despite the success, life could still prove tempestuous.

On 19 May the group were booked to appear on

Despite appearances, Kenney Jones never lived in Pimlico.

Kenney Jones in Westmoreland Terrace, 1966.

McLagan sorting out the tunes in Westmoreland Terrace, 1966.

Top Of The Pops, but following a dispute over billing they pulled out. Five days previously, a similar scene had occurred on ABC's *Thank Your Lucky Stars*, when the band were refused permission to play two songs.

'We refused to do *Lucky Stars* because although we had a bestselling LP out and a single in the charts, they refused to let us do more than one number and they wanted us to open the show which was being topped by Dee Dee Warwick.'

STEVE MARRIOTT, SUMMER 1966

Their refusal to be dictated to by anyone also extended to their live work. In the sixties, groups were often sent out on the road as a package. With a bestselling album and three hit singles behind them, The Small Faces, not unnaturally, expected top-billing status. When it was denied them, they simply refused to play.

A week after their run-in with *Top Of The Pops*, the show's producers relented and the group made their debut on one of Britain's longest running pop shows. It was to be the start of a stormy relationship which reached its zenith when

'Wouldn't it be nice to get on wiv me neighbours?' Westmoreland Terrace, 1966.

65

STEVE MARRIOTT'S offer to drop in and see The Small Faces at home sounded too good to miss, so Fiona and I made our way down to their house in South London.

Kenny Jones answered our knock at the door and he politely ushered us down to the room in the basement of the house that The Faces use for their general living quarters. Steve, dressed in a silk dressing gown, sat in front of a glowing electric fire.

"Mornin' folks," he said. "Sorry it's a bit chilly in here but our central heating has broken down.

"I had rather a late night and as it was so cold I just couldn't face the thought of climbing into freezing sheets so I stayed down here. Wasn't bad at all."

"'Fraid Plonk and Ian aren't up yet," said Kenny, "I'll go and give 'em a yell."

A few minutes later he returned with the news that Plonk had braved the cold and was on his way down but Ian was still snoring away.

"Why don't you take him a cuppa," said Steve, "that should make him move!"

Up we went to Ian's bedroom, where, from under a mass of sheets and blankets, we heard some rather strange noises that sounded awfully like snores!

"Mac," I said, "we've bought you a lovely, steaming cup of tea."

"It's a dream—it must be a dream," came the muffled reply, "nobody ever brings me tea in bed."

Slowly from under the clothes appeared a mod hair style followed by a small (sleepy) face.

"Good morning, people," said Ian. "Oh, it's true then, you have brought me some tea."

He did his best to dodge the photos that Fiona was taking, complaining that nobody would surely want to see him in this state, and we left him happily sipping his tea, and feeling

"We've moved into a new pad," said Small Face Steve Marriott. "You must drop in and see us." So, that's exactly what FAB's photographer Fiona and Doug Perry did! Here's all the gen they found on . . .

THE FACES

rather proud of ourselves for doing our good deed for the day.

Meanwhile downstairs Plonk had joined the other two and they sat around chatting while an Otis Redding disc hummed quietly away in the background. Steve talked a little about their new home.

"It's great," he said. "See, the thing is it's so convenient being together all the time cause we can discuss our act and try new things out on the spur of the moment, not have to wait and arrange a rehearsal. By the way, I must give you a bit of a guided tour round before you go.

Noises from the kitchen told us that Ian was up and he came in and began sorting through some of the enormous pile of fan mail the boys had received that day.

"Hey, there's one here from Nigeria," he said eagerly. "Wonder how they knew the address?"

"This one says that in Luton there's a new dance craze started called 'The Steve' named after Steve's stage movements," added Kenny.

"Cor, what a gas," said Steve. "Honestly, lovely new things like that are always happening. They knock me out!"

"I feel in a party mood," said Plonk. "Let's have a party."

I reminded him that it was eleven o'clock in the morning, not really party time.

"Don't worry," he answered, dancing around the room to the beat of the record, "any time's party time for me."

"Come and have a look round," said Steve leading us through the kitchen and up to the ground floor of the house.

It's a great place The Small Faces have. There are four storeys and three or four rooms on each floor. Besides the boys' bedrooms there's a room that they use for rehearsals, another one where they store all their spare gear and in another room they have a fantastic model racing track set out. Steve's bedroom is on the top floor and a passage from it leads you to a bathroom which houses hot and cold showers.

"That's my waking up room," he said, pointing to the bathroom. "I roll out of bed and go straight under the shower. It's a bit ickyboo at first, but I feel great when I come out. All sort of wide-awake and ready to entertain any friends who pop round."

Well, we certainly had our fun at The Small Faces' house, and if you turn to page 20 you'll find that YOU might get the chance to go and visit the boys, too. The winners of our Small Faces competition are to be invited round to have tea with Steve, Kenny, Plonk and Ian. I'll tell you something—they'll have a great time.

DOUG PERRY

Steve tells his early morning troubles to one of his gonk friends "Big Louis."

"No milk again," says Kenny. "Oh well, black coffee's better than none at all."

"Plonk's" day always starts with a wash of his locks and a look at the mail.

Did you ever see anyone who enjoyed a shave as much as "Plonk"?

Could be the makings of a new hit song that Steve is playing on his guitar.

Ian has that let-me-get-at-it look as he takes his cuppa. Hope he enjoyed it!

"This pile of fan mail gets bigger and bigger every day," says Steve, happily.

Small Face in action. Ian dances to the disc playing on the gram.

The press come to Pimlico. Within a year the group would have separate pads.

Marriott insulted the show's producer, Johnny Stewart.

'I thought this particular producer [Stewart] was leaving the show,' he recalled, 'and this other guy, Colin Charman, who was the floor manager, was taking over. Anyway, after we had done our bit, this producer comes into the bar, and he was doing this thing of, "That was wonderful, lads, it was a gas, it was wild." Really full of shit. I knew he did it with everyone whether he liked you or not. So I turned around and said, "You're a cunt, a real two-faced cunt." And he wasn't leaving the show at all. It was, "Oh wrong!"'

Another victim of Marriott's refusal to form superficial relationships with industry figures was a young Tony Blackburn.

'Every time I spoke to him,' Marriott recalled, 'I would call him a different name. I'd call him Simon, Eamonn or any other DJ's name but never his own. Anyway, I wanted to give him a cabbage to let him know what I thought of him. So I'm calling him all these different names and at the same time he's holding this cabbage and doesn't quite know why he's got it. It hasn't dawned on him yet and as it slowly dawns on him what a cunt he looks holding this cabbage he went mad and offered me outside. "Come outside!" he's shouting, and all his make-up is running. He was shouting, "You little cunt, you'll never work at the BBC again." I was crying with laughter.'

Mac sports the pork-pie hat look. Pimlico, circa 1966.

In June, with 'Hey Girl' still in the charts, the group finished a week-long engagement in Scotland and then flew south to appear on Ready Steady Go. The schedule was too much. At the TV studios, Marriott collapsed from low blood pressure. He was taken back to Pimlico and ordered to rest.

The collapse was the culmination of the group's non-stop work schedule, and it wasn't only Marriott who was suffering. Glyn Johns was so concerned by Lane's obvious physical deterioration that he insisted

Kenney with his MGA sports car, circa 1966.

the bassist stay at his flat for a few days to recuperate. No one was told of Lane's whereabouts.

Five days later business resumed with the group appearing at the Top Rank, Sunderland. They played six more UK dates and then flew to Paris to appear on French TV. That Marriott had regained his health and devil-may-care attitude was clearly in evidence from his antics in Paris.

'We ended up having this huge row with the show's producers because it was totally disorganised,' Jones recalls. 'All these cameras bumping into each other and, from where I was sitting, they looked like bumper cars. I couldn't stop laughing. But something happened and our road manager wouldn't let us do what the producer wanted, which was something stupid. So in the end we walked off. Steve crept up and nicked the master reel of the whole show because we didn't want to be on it, and there's Steve running down the road in Paris with this big reel under his arm laughing his head off. We caused havoc.'

Despite this carefree attitude, on a musical level success seemed to have a positive rather than a negative effect on the group. Although they had little in common with those who worked in the music business, and were both rattled and frustrated by their teeny-bop image, Marriott and Lane's songwriting partnership was blossoming, as their impending single was about to prove.

'They complemented themselves as writers incredibly,' Johns points out. 'Ronnie on his own or Steve on his own were half the combination of the two together.'

In July The Small Faces had been placed eighth in the NME poll, and at the beginning of August Rave magazine handed over their issue to the group to produce a one-off special.

A couple of days later, on 5 August 1966, 'All Or Nothing'/'Understanding' was released.

'We're progressing all the time. Even "All Or Nothing" has moved along, which is a gas. "Sha La La" and "Hey Girl" were really nursery rhymes. We're now writing lyrics that mean something and it'll be great . . . I was getting typecast vocally, the same as we were before we broke away with "All Or Nothing".'

STEVE MARRIOTT, AUGUST 1966

'"All Or Nothing" was getting us to where we wanted to be musically,' Kenney Jones explains. 'It wasn't as poppy but it was still commercial. It was an all-round better song than anything we had done until then, it was breaking us out of the pop system.'

'We were in the studio doing two songs, one of them mine, and one Plonk's. Our manager Don Arden didn't like the sound of either of them and we hadn't got anything else. So Plonk said, "Play him that tune you were working out." Don was knocked out and gave us two bits of paper and we wrote the lyrics in half an hour. It was all at an LP session and this song wasn't even on the agenda.'

STEVE MARRIOTT ON 'ALL OR NOTHING', AUGUST 1966

Produced by Don Arden, this was the first truly classic Small Faces single, marked by a persuasive

Don Arden added a year to McLagan's birthdate when he first joined the group.

melody and Marriott's forceful vocal performance. It deservedly gave them their first number one – of **sorts. On 15 September it replaced The Beatles'** insipid 'Yellow Submarine' at the top spot, but not before a draw had been called.

'We were actually joint number one,' Jones recalls. 'Top Of The Pops showed a picture that week of both us and The Beatles with all our faces joined together. Like there was half of me and half of Ringo joined together. Half of Steve and half of John (Lennon) and so on. It was a first joint number one and it's never happened since.'

vehicle, banging on the roof and bonnet. Their combined weight began to push the car into the soft ground, while inside all the group could do was try to hold up the roof with their hands and watch helplessly as squirming teenage faces, pushing up against the window, disappeared from view.

When the fans were finally cleared, one had broken a leg under the car's wheels. The group, shaken beyond belief, left the stadium, drove away and then ordered their driver to stop. They got out and reportedly ran for two miles through a nearby field, screaming their heads off.

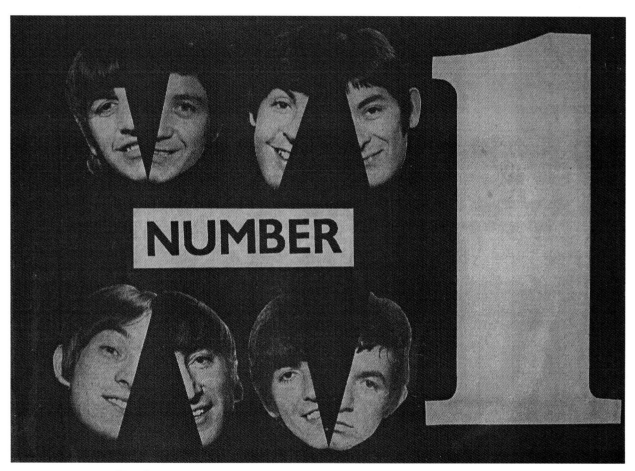

The Small Faces tie with The Beatles at number one, September 1966.

The single's huge success was to trigger even wilder scenes of teen hysteria. At Oldham Football Club the group made an appearance in front of thousands of fans as part of a charity match. Just before kick-off, they were driven to the middle of the pitch in an old Vauxhall car. On seeing them, the fans broke through security and surrounded the

'We found this disused railway line,' Jones recalls, 'and we just let rip. That's when I realised how close we were.'

In Glasgow, Lane and McLagan made the mistake of being caught outside their hotel by fans. Lane was knocked out and McLagan escorted to the local police station where he spent the night, 'for his own safety'.

When a SMALL FACE spent a night behind bars . . .

by STEVE MARRIOTT

HELP! All us SMALL FACES are still shaking after the riots we suffered in Glasgow last Thursday night which ended with Ian McLagan spending the night in a police cell!

When we got back to our hotel after the show, we were besieged by fans. Kenny and I managed to get inside to safety, "Plonk" was battered about and had to be dragged inside, but Ian got locked out and the police "arrested" him for his own safety and he spent the night on a cell bed.

This tour—our second major one—is too fantastic for words. The reception has been unbelievable.

My favourite is NEIL CHRISTIAN with whom I've had several long chats. What a nice guy he is, and he's got a great stage act.

Mac reckons CRISPIAN ST. PETERS gave him the biggest surprise. After reading lots of criticism of Crispian, he's proved he's not all mouth and can really sing.

We all think the KOOBAS could easily get a hit record and be very big.

After opening at Lewisham we went back to our house for a celebration party, but we had no food and drink and had to make do with coffee.

I think "Plonk" is worried. If he gets any thinner, he'll have to run round in a shower if he wants to get wet.

I hope you see us when we visit your town. —Love, STEVE.

Marriott appeals for calm, autumn 1966.

After the success of both album and single, the group's future looked decidedly rosy – at least from the outside. From the inside it was a different story. If the fans' behaviour masked the group's musical skills, leaving them increasingly agitated, it also brought home to them how successful they were. Yet the money they were receiving in no way mirrored this success.

'We were playing every night of the week,' Jones recalls, 'and we were still only getting twenty pounds a week. So we started to complain. Don had said, "I'll look after the money from the gigs, I don't want you to look after it or take it away with you." Which was all right to start with, until we started playing so many.

'So we complained and he gave us sixty pounds a week. We were doing things like double gigs where we'd earn six hundred pounds, sometimes a grand, which was an awful lot of money in those days – twelve hundred to two grand, all around that mark.

'So Don said, "I'll open a bank account for you and put it all in there." We all walked up to this bank and he opened up an account, a Small Faces account with his signature as the sole signature, and that was the last we ever saw of that. I call that my apprenticeship to the music business. We would say to others for years after, "Don't do this, don't do that," and then we went and did it all over again at Immediate.'

News of a growing rift between the band and manager started to circulate within the music business. One man who heard these whispers was an employee of Robert Stigwood and he expressed an interest in managing the band. Don Arden's response, as chronicled in Starmakers and Svengalis, was not untypical.

'I had to stop these overtures – and quickly,' he is quoted as saying. 'I contacted two well-muscled friends and hired two more equally huge toughs. And we went along to nail this impresario to his chair with fright. There was a large ornate ashtray on his desk. I picked it up and smashed it down with such force that the desk cracked – giving a good impression of a man wild with rage. My friends and I had carefully rehearsed our next move. I pretended to go beserk, lifted the impresario bodily from his chair, dragged him to the balcony and held him so he was looking down to the pavement four floors below. I asked my friends if I should drop him or forgive him. In unison they shouted: "Drop him." He went rigid with shock and I thought he might have a heart attack. Immediately, I dragged him back into

In-store signing, circa 1966.

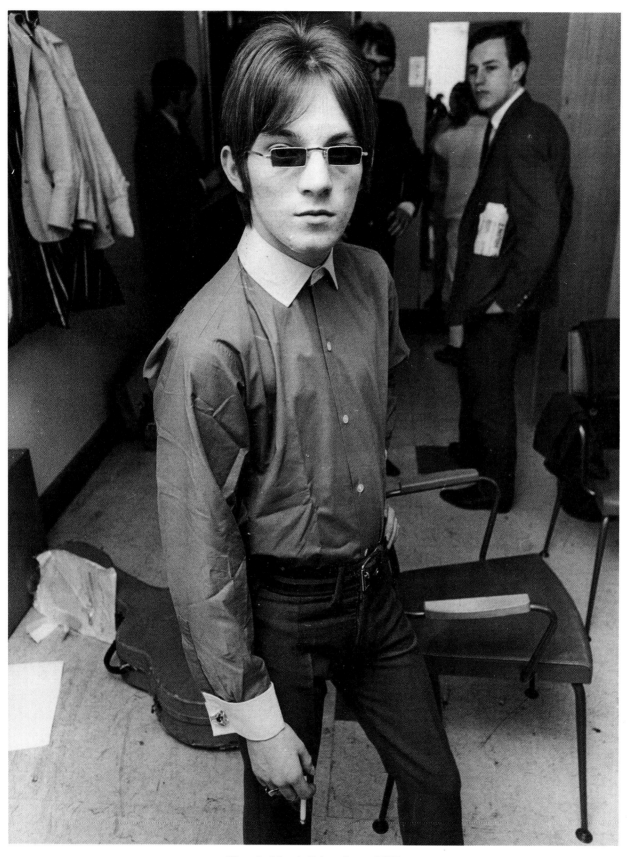

Classic Marriott, top face, 1966.

Thanks Everyone!

'All Or Nothing' at number one and the boys take a rare drink.

the room and warned him never to interfere with my groups again.'

On another occasion, Ronnie Lane went to talk to Arden about money. As soon as he entered the manager's office he was introduced to 'Mad Tom', one of Arden's assistants. The message came through that perhaps Lane should return another day. Marriott was to have a similar experience with 'Mad Tom', forming the basis for a song he would write the following year for the group's final album.

Further trouble ensued when Arden himself called in the band's parents for an unexpected meeting at his office. According to Kenney Jones, the manager was worried about the group's drug intake, which now included hefty amounts of LSD.

'I didn't take the stuff,' says Jones, 'but the others did. The only time I took it was down at Portland Studios when Marriott spiked my drink. All I could do was say, "Look at my left hand, look at my left hand," as I was playing drums that night.'

Drugs, particularly LSD, had been around the group since the move to Pimlico. It was taken primarily to induce creativity. 'We took acid very seriously,' Lane says. (In a recent interview, Lane asked this author if he had ever taken acid. On being told no, Lane replied, 'Well you should take some, man, especially if you're going to write my book!')

Arden, who was from an older generation, couldn't understand the drug's attraction. What's more, a band who are constantly stoned are less likely to meet their commitments, and therefore more likely to lose money. He decided to squeal on the band in an attempt to jolt them out of their drug taking. He told the parents that the group were frittering away hundreds of pounds on illegal substances. Shocked and very worried, the parents left Arden's office in a state of understandable panic and confronted their sons that night.

Naturally, it took some time before the four musicians could persuade their parents – who, on the band's insistence, were also receiving twenty pounds a week – that they were not drug addicts.

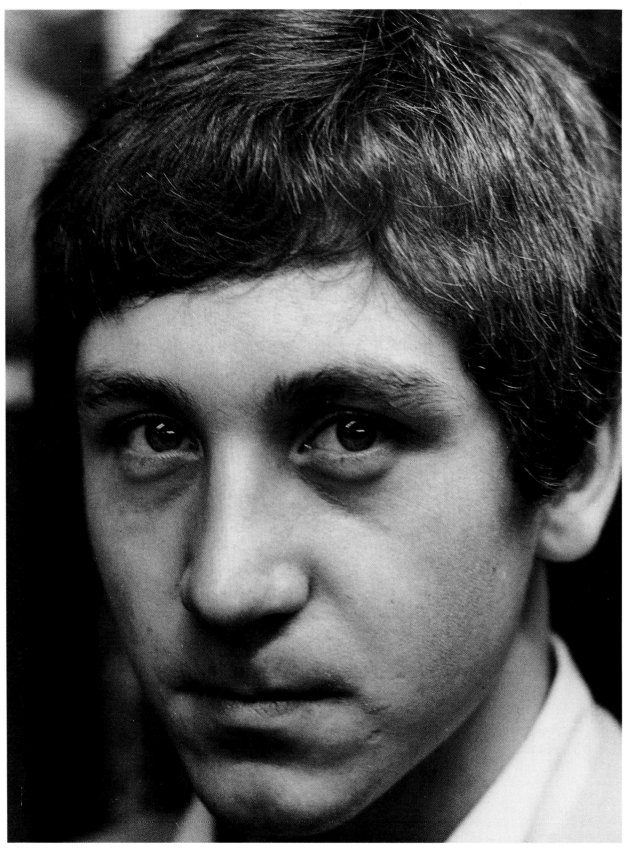

Kenney Jones' East End look

Black and white photo from July 1966 for *Valentine* magazine.

'It was such a nasty thing to do,' Jones states. 'We really hated him after that.'

'In the beginning,' Lane recalls, 'when I trusted him, I thought he was a wonderful guy. Then he did all that stuff with the drugs. Of course, my father, Big Stan, he smoked a bit of hashish himself so it didn't mean nothing to him.'

With a prestigious number one under their belts, Arden then announced to the press that The Small Faces would tour the States in December, following a short US TV and radio promotional stint. Both trips failed to materialise and Glyn Johns now believes this was the band's biggest mistake.

'That was the key,' he asserts. 'If they had gone to America they would have absolutely cleaned up. When English bands went to America in the sixties and made it, immediately their standing in Great Britain was tripled. That never happened with The Small Faces.'

The official reason, put out later by Arden, for the band's failure to play in the States was that Ian McLagan had a previous drug conviction (possession of cannabis) and had been refused entry. In fact, McLagan now says, that was just a smoke-screen.

'Arden announced that American tour but he didn't want us to go. He was scared that we would meet with American agents or managers and find out how much money we should have been getting. So he offered us this four-month tour on a bus with all these other groups, knowing full well that we would say no way. When I did get busted [the following year, November 1967] that was given out as the reason.'

More frustration ensued when the group were booked on to an October package tour featuring The Hollies and The Nashville Teens. Due to another billing dispute, the band started pulling out of gigs and the tour nosedived into chaos. For the first time The Small Faces felt the wrath of the music press.

'No matter how right The [Small] Faces feel they were in terms of contract, I reckon that morally they were wrong in that they failed in their obligation to the fans,' thundered the NME.

Instead, the group began work on their second

album while Arden flew to the States to try to arrange a two-week Christmas spectacular, to be held at the Hammersmith Odeon, which would also feature a couple of American groups, The Mamas and the Papas and The Lovin' Spoonful.

Again, the idea was a non-starter. Matters reached boiling point when Decca, impatient for a follow-up to the group's number one single, released, without their knowledge or permission, 'My Mind's Eye'/'I Can't Dance With You'.

Arden, who was anxious that the group release a single before Christmas, had been badgering them to start recording. To placate him, they had sent him a rough demo of 'My Mind's Eye', to prove that any worries he might have about their abilities, especially in the wake of the recent drugs and parents debacle, were totally unfounded.

'It's great. Fabulous. Records are made to be criticised. We love it. "My Mind's Eye" was originally recorded as an album track but the powers that be decided it should be issued as a single. Sure, we nicked it. Someone somewhere said the bloke who wrote the song would be turning in his grave if he heard "My Mind's Eye" – but I'm sure he'd be leaping about. I'll certainly be chuffed if someone revives one of our songs in a couple of years.'

STEVE MARRIOTT, ON THE SIMILARITY BETWEEN 'GLORIA IN EXCELSIS' AND 'MY MIND'S EYE', DECEMBER 1966

Somehow the tape fell into Decca's hands.

'The first time we heard it was on the car radio,' Marriott recalled. 'We were driving home or to some gig up North and it just came on, "Here's the latest single by The Small Faces." Everyone was WHAT!'

'My Mind's Eye' was another artistic step forward, but it was the B-side, 'I Can't Dance With You', that must have excited those fans who instinctively understood the group's mission.

The latter song lasts three minutes and twelve

seconds and captures with breathtaking excitement The Small Faces in a powerful and raw phase. Kenney Jones' drums are way up in the mix (not unlike much of today's hip-hop recordings), his playing propelling the song along in a furious flurry of crashing cymbals. McLagan's organ stabs are used repetitively while Lane's bass zooms in and out, anchoring down Marriott's dark, powerful vocals until he slides into the song's chorus. It was a record that easily fulfilled their ambition to produce the authenticity of Black R & B and align it with their own musical sensibilities.

The single may have reached number four in the charts but in terms of the band's relationship with both manager and record company, the end was clearly in sight. The boys had already appointed an independent lawyer to look into their financial affairs so it was no surprise when at Christmas 1966 it was announced that they and Arden had agreed to go their separate ways.

'I'm not well off, none of us are. We live pretty comfortably but we are by no means rich. We know a bit more now about what's going on around us financially. When we came head-first into the business we were so green and there were so many con-men around.'

STEVE MARRIOTT, MAY 1967

The argument over money, however, would drag well into the next year. In the summer of 1967 the group brought an action against Contemporary Music for royalties owing. In October, the case went to court and the judge ruled in the group's favour. A week after this victory they received a letter from Arden's solicitors stating that he had insufficient funds to pay the money [£4023 and 7 shillings] in full. Instead, it was proposed that he pay a monthly sum of £250. Contemporary Records paid two instalments and then abrubtly ceased payments.

It was not until ten years later that the group finally managed to retrieve all the money owed to them.

Ian Patrick McLagan, rather handsome.

SMALL FACES

Immediate promo card for the band's second album.

1967: DON'T BURST MY BUBBLE

By the year The Beatles released *Sgt Pepper's Lonely Hearts Club Band*, the Mod movement was on its last well-tailored legs. *Ready Steady Go* was finished and the Flamingo had closed down. Once Modernism had meant sharp clothes and cool attitudes, but over the last three years it had degenerated into an unseemly morass of Bank Holiday scuffles with rockers, which had been partly encouraged by media sensationalism.

The whole Mod movement looked and felt undignified. It was too large, too unwieldy and, worst of all, a contradiction in terms. How can you have an élitist mass movement?

If anything summed up its downfall it was the switch of emphasis that occurred in drug culture. The choice of a new generation was not amphetamines but their counterparts, LSD and marijuana.

It was the middle-class kids, the students and the drop-outs, inspired by the hippie movement in San Francisco, who had seized the middle ground from the Mods and imposed their new values of peace and love. Pop music changed accordingly. Especially with the arrival of *Sgt Pepper*.

Taking their cue from this obviously drug-influenced work, the groups started to abandon the tight three-minute structure and explore lengthy musical avenues. One of these groups was The Pink Floyd who were often to be found at the UFO club in Tottenham Court Road, playing long gigs with suitably 'trippy' light shows to augment the sound. When a Mod spotted Pete Townshend at that very same club, checking out the Floyd in his flares and beads, he knew for sure that an era had just died.

What was ironic, as one writer noted, was that groups such as the Floyd were actually more into alcohol than mind-bending chemicals. It was the teeny-bopper groups, such as The Small Faces, who were busy guzzling down large quantities of LSD. Despite their various references to dope in interviews, it was this thinking that allowed The Small Faces to escape being heavily linked to the drug scene. Other groups weren't so fortunate.

'I wonder what the Government would do if somebody invented spirits today? If they invented whiskey today, they would ban it. I know a lot of people who smoke and they are all beautiful people. Old Bill should leave it alone. What do they think they are going to do – stop it?'

STEVE MARRIOTT, APRIL 1967

Flower Power makes its mark on the boys' shirts.

This then was the beginning of Flower Power and the concerted attempt by the British establishment to stamp it out. Groups such as The Rolling Stones, who at the time were busy flaunting their rebel image, were placed under heavy surveillance by both the media and the police. The group's nucleus – Brian Jones, Mick Jagger and Keith Richards – paid the price with numerous court appearances and suspended prison sentences.

A rock underground had now sprung up and begun to make its presence felt. This underground, which consisted of middle-class drop-outs, considered straightahead pop music meaningless. The pop single was trite and not worth the vinyl it was printed on. Singles were for kids, albums were for 'intellectuals'. This influence can be gauged by the fact that in 1967 albums outsold singles for the first time ever.

To be a credible, respected musician you had to win the approval of this audience and, for a working-class group from the East End who were considered 'pop stars', the relationship was never going to be easy. The Small Faces detested this network as much as they did their bosses at Decca.

For Marriott and Co., who had been taking LSD for at least two years by this time, psychedelic music was a valid genre, but to their ears no one had successfully incorporated it into their music. To them, the records that were now emerging had little depth and carried none of the excitement that makes music so special.

The group's ambition now was to introduce psychedelia into their work while never losing sight of their main strengths – melody, lyrics and structure.

Accordingly, many of the middle-class led media viewed their work from this period as a typical east London attempt to take the mickey. The band's penchant for 'jokey type' songs served to negate their actual artistic breakthroughs. With psychedelia, the group were trying to show the way forward by

'We started out as ravers. On stage we're still limited and have to make the best of what we've got – at the moment anyway. Basically our stage act is the same as it was two years ago, which isn't a good thing. But you, the fans, dig it, so it's all right. We were ravers and pretty things used to make us sick. We had no time for them. Now we're on the way to the soft extreme but at the moment we're in the middle, which is nice. We'd like to stay here for a while. It's only just begun and we'll flow along with it.'

STEVE MARRIOTT, WRITING IN THE MUSIC PRESS, JUNE 1967

incorporating it into their records without making it the main focus. Their efforts were never truly recognised. Too many people either expected laughs or were cynical that such a group could be so inventive.

With the loss of their first manager, The Small Faces now entered their second and most productive phase. Arden had sold the group for a reputed £12,000 to the Harold Davidson Group, a division of the Lew Grade Organisation.

In January and February, as contracts flew here, there and everywhere, The Small Faces took comfort from the *NME*'s Christmas poll which confirmed their popularity by placing them sixth in the Best British Vocal Group category and voting 'All Or Nothing' the sixth best single of 1966. Marriott came thirteenth and fourth respectively in the same paper's Best British Vocal Personality and New Disc Singer categories. While this was perhaps the best news to come the band's way for a long time, the managerial disputes raged on.

Arguments over touring plans with Harold Davidson and Tito Burns (the agent whom the group detested as the epitome of music business flashness, with his suits and cigars) ensured that for January and February The Small Faces were holed up in Olympic Studios, writing and recording.

Among the new material was one song, 'My Way Of Giving', that was handed over to recording vocalist Chris Farlowe, who had hit big, four singles previously, with 'Out Of Time' (written by Jagger and Richards). Released on 27 January, it was the

first of a series of songs Marriott and Lane wrote for artists on Andrew Loog Oldham's Immediate label. The single went into the UK charts at forty-eight but the next week dropped out.

'That all came about,' Marriott recalled, 'from a blind date I did for *Melody Maker*. [This was a spot in the paper where musicians were played singles then asked their opinion, without knowing who the artist was.] Immediate had been going for a while and one of their records came up and I said, "I like the way Andrew produces."

'He got hold of me after that and said, "Let's have a natter about what you're doing." I knew him from way back and he said he was interested in working with us and did we have any songs?'

The midgets strike back.

81

Mirabelle's
Pat
Saville
says

happiness is a SMALL FACE

● Small Faces, left to right: 'Plonk' Lane, Kenny Jones, Steve Marriot and Ian McLagan.

ATTENTION all Small Faces fans. The group needs your help!

It's not your money they're after — it's empty egg boxes.

Yes, incredible as it may seem, it's those little papier maché cases they want and unless they get some help they will be eating eggs for breakfast, dinner and tea for quite a while just to get enough egg boxes.

When Plonk asked if I knew where he could get some I thought at first it was all part of the group's "looning around" (the boys' own description of their more crazy ideas and antics). But no, they were perfectly serious.

What are the egg boxes needed for?

"They're to line the walls and ceiling of a room in my new flat," explained Plonk.

The thought of this being a new form of op-art interior decoration made me want to "fall about" as the group would say, but somehow I managed not to laugh.

It was just as well for Plonk went on to say, "I'm converting the room into a recording studio and the egg boxes will make it soundproof. The only trouble is that we need such a lot, so if anyone has some to spare I will be pleased to take them off their hands."

Trust the Small Faces to come up with such a great idea.

Like other groups they have the use of official recording studios but they explained that these are heavily booked.

"We can't always use them just when we want to but if we can make a studio we will be able to produce our own demo-discs and spend more time working on new ideas," said Plonk.

This is just one of the Small Faces' new ventures but it will play an important part in their musical progression. Since their fantastic rise to fame they've had many hit records but are obviously not content with their success as performers. In recent months their thoughts have been turning more and more towards writing numbers for themselves and other stars.

"For a long time it's been one of our ambitions to write something for Chris Farlowe and now with 'My Way of Giving', we've done it," said Steve with a note of satisfaction in his voice.

Writing comes easily to Steve and Plonk but Mac finds it more difficult.

"I've got the ideas, only they never get off the ground. But I'll keep on trying and perhaps I'll manage it one day," he said optimistically.

Steve talked enthusiastically about their latest discs.

We're wild about our new single 'I Can't Make It'. It's the best thing we've done. We're also very pleased with our latest L.P. It's got some great new sounds and we've even used a harpsichord in some of the numbers. That's something we couldn't have done a year ago, but now that we're more established we have a greater say in what we record."

The Small Faces are one of the most popular groups on the British scene but Steve admits that fame can be a dangerous thing.

"It alters your whole life and way of looking at things. The worst part is when you start believing the glowing reports about yourself in the papers. I went through a stage like that when 'Sha-la-la-la-lee' was number one. I soon got over it but even now

I feel ashamed to think that I ever thought I was someone special."

Fame has had little effect on Kenny, who still lives with his family in a small house in London's East End. The only outward indications of his new prosperity are his shining sports car and his horse Pedro Jones, which is stabled in Essex. He seems to regret the loss of old friends.

"Whenever I see them they make cracks about me being big headed. I don't think I am. I'm sure I haven't changed, it's their attitude towards me that has and it makes me feel very embarrassed when we meet."

Fame may have made Kenny even more shy and quiet but as for it making him big-headed, that's the one effect it certainly hasn't had.

Now that they have been on the scene for almost two years what do The Small Faces think of the newcomers to the pop world?

"I think The Monkees are very lucky boys," said Steve. He added that although both he and Davy Jones had appeared in the London stage production of "Oliver!" they were not in the show at the same time, so had never met.

But it was Jimi Hendrix who came in for the greatest praise from Steve.

"In this business you sometimes wonder if anything new and exciting will ever come along and then from nowhere someone like Jimi appears. I went to see him at the Saville Theatre—he was fantastic. I stood and cheered. It was the first time in years that I felt like a fan!"

When a top group like The Small Faces can pay other artistes such sincere compliments it's a sure sign that their own success hasn't gone to their heads—and that is very nice to know.

✱ Send Plonk's egg boxes to
THE SMALL FACES FAN CLUB,
REGENT HOUSE,
235 REGENT STREET, LONDON, W.1.

Marriott praises Hendrix and Lane appeals for empty egg boxes – all is as it should be.

Marriott and Lane's second offering was 'Tell Me Have You Ever Seen Me' which was given to The Apostolic Intervention, a little-known group that had signed to Immediate under the name RAF. Marriott was suitably impressed by their music although he hated their moniker. He suggested they change it to The Nice, after a song he had just written entitled 'Here Come The Nice'. Andrew Loog Oldham rejected the idea. But three weeks later he named singer P. P. Arnold's backing group . . . The Nice.

The Apostolic Intervention's only known member was Jerry Shirley on drums, with whom Marriott would later form Humble Pie. Marriott sang backing vocals on the track as well as co-producing with Ronnie Lane. The single, however, failed to chart.

'We discovered little Jerry Shirley,' Jones recalls, 'when he used to come and watch us as a kid in short trousers. We're all on that session but it's so hard to tell whose drumming because Jerry would sit and scrutinise my drumming all the time and copy it beat for beat.

'We were doing a lot of session work at the time. Steve and Ronnie were getting into producing and writing for other people because Andrew was encouraging us and taking a lot of interest. He saw that we weren't just a pop band.

'I was doing some sessions for Immediate with Mike D'Abo, and one of the tracks that came out of that was "First Cut Is The Deepest" by P. P. Arnold. We finished that and a couple more with just me and Mike on piano, and Rod Stewart came in a week later and sung on another track which turned out to be "Little Miss Understood". That's what it was like. We were all in and out of each other's studios, having a play on this or that or someone would come in and play on our stuff.'

On 28 January, the band took part in Radio Luxembourg's Battle of the Bands, beating Manfred Mann in the final.

Later that night, they dropped in on a Rolling Stones recording session, despite the rumours that Marriott was now seeing Jagger's ex-girlfriend, model Chrissie Shrimpton.

'It was probably a bit of a rebound thing,' Marriott noted. 'I don't know. I had a great time with her. What happened was that she did the odd

Receiving the Battle of the Bands award from Jackie Trent, 1967.

Steve and Chrissie Shrimpton. 'A rebound thing.'

a big family thing up at Immediate. There were only about four or five acts on the label. Admittedly all charting, but only a handful of people were responsible for it all, so everyone got to know each other very well. Everyone was connected to everyone else in some way. It was inevitable that these things should crop up.'

For The Small Faces, managerial troubles still persisted. Harold Davidson had by now booked them on a package tour – scheduled to start in March – that would feature Roy Orbison and Paul and Barry Ryan.

Before it could get underway, The Small Faces, unsurprisingly, dumped Tito Burns as their agent. They then worked with Robert Wace, who temporarily managed them, before finally signing a long-term management deal with Immediate. (Decca were still to license their records.)

'We wanted to go to Immediate,' Marriott explained, 'because Andrew offered us every freedom, besides being a management company,

'Six months ago life was a drag. We all had our chins on the floor. We had no real enthusiasm in the records we were making and we did gig after gig, life was just monotonous. Then came the move to Immediate and it was just like a kick up the pants for us. We started getting better songs to record. Like "Itchycoo Park" for example.'

STEVE MARRIOTT, AUTUMN 1967

secretarial work for Andrew up at Immediate. We all fancied her a bit and she came to the Albert Hall when The Small Faces did a gig there. She came back to the house afterwards and copped hold of me.

'She and Mick were still talking and ringing each other up but that's about all. The papers went mad about it, loads of articles, and Mick rang up complaining, so I had to get on the phone and say, no, she never said this, I never said that, because we didn't. It was typical press stuff.

'She ended up running a kids' nursery. It was such

although not a very good one I might add. Their interest was selling records and nothing more than being a record label. They had sus and they knew that if they let us loose and gave us the reins then we would write better material and last a lot longer. Andrew knew we could and would write stuff that lasted for ever which, quite frankly, a lot of it has and still will. They were very shrewd people in that sense. It was a good move.'

'We met Andrew [Loog Oldham] when we were doing a tour of Europe. We got to Zurich and met him. He gives us a free hand and we all get on that way.'

STEVE MARRIOTT, 1967

POP ROMANCE?

RAVE's Dawn James speaks to Steve Marriott and Chrissie Shrimpton to find out just how true the rumours are about their pop romance!

"Yes" says Steve

It started as the old year was dying and 1967 promised hope. Chrissie Shrimpton just off with the old love Mick Jagger, was unwittingly reaching out towards the new one—Steve Marriott. She walked along a London street gay and unremorseful, and Steve walked beside her. "Go away" she giggled, "I look stupid next to you, you're so small."

"No, it's because you're so big" he responded.

"You look like a little Chinese man" she said.

"Your left eye is larger than your right one" he said.

"You remind me of my little brother, and he gets spanked" she said.

"Go on then, I dare you" he said, and there was a chase along the road.

A surprising way for a fairly serious relationship to start? It depends on how well you understand the characters involved. There is a romance between Chrissie and Steve, they both admit it.

Chrissie is a gay person, who depends on being happy.

This attracted Steve, who surrounds himself with gaiety. She is a kind person, who will be having a lovely time and see one of the party isn't, and say "Oh! you aren't enjoying it, let's do something else." She is a person who admits, "I'm no one, I'm Jean's sister and Mick's ex, and Steve's current". But there is a quality in her that has landed her two of the most eligible catches in pop. What is it?

"She is an own-up" Steve said, "which makes a change." It is not cool to be honest, to be cool you have to like everyone. Chrissie doesn't and says so. She is easy-going. She doesn't demand engagement rings, or the safety of the bonds of marriage.

"She loves animals, and life, and people." Steve said "Chrissie has a warmth for people and she attracts them to her. They tell her their troubles and she tries to help.

"She's the kind of girl you are loathe to hurt because she gets upset if you do."

This quality Mick saw in Chrissie too. Once at an after-the-show party Mick was leaving the room to telephone Chrissie who was at home in London.

"Use this phone Mick," someone offered. "No" Mick said "She might get upset if she heard all the noise. I'd rather not risk it."

Chrissie is not a limelight stealer, which may be why she attracts such great personalities as Mick and Steve.

"She is not the kind of girl everyone gapes at" Steve said. "She prefers to stay in the background. She is happy for the bloke she is out with to be the one on show. That's nice. She doesn't take part in my music as such, tends to ignore me when I'm digging a sound, but I take her to all my sessions because she is good for me as a person and that helps my music.

"She is a laugh, easy-going, if a session goes wrong, she just says, let's go home and invite friends round and forget, tomorrow it will be good."

Chrissie is the first girlfriend Steve has admitted to. Why? "It was own-up Chrissie Shrimpton time" he said, "I didn't particularly want publicity on it, but it would have been most uncool to refuse to comment to the press, because we are going together, we are very happy. I don't have any plans. Marriage, I don't know about it. It is so soon. We are just enjoying knowing each other. We need time, but she is a wonderful girl."

"Yes" says Chrissie

Chrissie complies with the average modern image, groovy mini-skirts, long, brown hair, and a wardrobe full of plums and browns and blacks. She faces life as Jean's sister, and the girlfriend of Mick and Steve, and she genuinely doesn't like it. When she goes to clubs, more often than not she uses a false name. "I get so sick at being stared at" she said. "It's all so silly, I haven't done anything great. I am not a top model. Or a big pop star. I don't want to be. I am not ambitious, I just want to be left in peace to be happy."

She still drives a mini car given to her by Mick. "It has only got a driver's seat and half a back seat, the others were pinched by fans," she said, remembering the time when she wasn't left in peace. She lived in the siege of Mick's fans for years. Do Steve's fans bother her so much? "No, not at all. They are very friendly and sweet, they put letters through the door wishing me luck and happiness with Steve."

She and Steve have a lot in common. They share a love of cats and horses. "Steve didn't used to like cats, but he is very fond of them now. He has got one called Grace. And I've got one, and they get on fine. Stevie had a birthday party on January 30th and we got him a beautiful cake. But Grace got at it first." Things like that make Chrissie laugh. She has a schoolgirl quality, she laughs too loud and leaps about on long legs not caring how she looks. She likes to curl up on a bed and chatter nonsense, while Stevie is digging a sound. "I'm not at all cool" she tells people with a twinkle in her eye. "I'm an own-up, what a drag."

And she roared with laughter.

The pop star and the model. The tradition continues.

The band's new manager was, undoubtedly, one of the decade's key figures. Born in 1944, by the time he was eleven Andrew Loog Oldham was hanging out in coffee bars, such as the famous Two Is, and witnessing the birth of 'the teenager'. It was to have a lasting effect on him. He left his public school with just a handful of O-levels and landed a

Lane was a gypsy and rustic romantic at heart.

job with Mary Quant, the brilliant designer who shaped that decade's fashions. In her biography, *Quant by Quant*, she recalls the young entrepreneur:

'Andrew can't have been little more than sixteen at the time: he had just left school but he had all the confidence in the world. Archie thought he was a very bright boy and did a lot to help him. One day Andrew confided in Archie's wife, Cathy, that he could do any of our jobs standing on his head (Archie's included). Cathy asked him what he did.

'"Well," he said, "when Mary's a bit tired, I design a few dresses for her; when Alexander is choosing stock, I chat up the press for him. I could do it just as well on my own. It's easy."

'Then, suddenly, entirely unexpectedly, we got a note from Andrew on Bazaar writing paper. It was his formal resignation posted at the airport as he was leaving the country. Archie heard of him a little later when he was apparently trying to get a job on *Time* magazine and the editor telephoned to find out whether anyone as young as Andrew could possibly have done all the things he claimed to have done. Nothing came of this but not long afterwards we heard that he had become manager of The Rolling Stones! Obviously he was right in all that he claimed. Even at sixteen he could have done any of our jobs.'

Before he got to the Stones, Oldham had briefly worked for both Don Arden and Brian Epstein. His idol was American producer Phil Spector (whose image – dark shades and suits – he adopted wholesale). Oldham vowed that one day he would follow him into production, but this ambition was soon forgotten when he realised that pop management offered an easier route to success.

In 1962, acting on a tip-off, he went down to the Station Hotel in Richmond and, in a growing state of excitement, watched The Rolling Stones perform to a packed house.

He charmed his way into their camp, ousted their acting manager, Giorgio Gomelsky, told pianist Ian Stewart that he was 'too ordinary to be a pop star', found a backer in one Eric Easton and signed the band to Decca.

He was determined that Jagger and Richards would equal Lennon and McCartney. So, after some chart success with covers such as 'Come On', he locked the pair in a room and ordered them to write.

Ironically, it was a cover – Bobby Womack's 'It's All Over Now' – that did the trick, unleashing the Stones and their unruly image on to an unsuspecting public. Oldham revelled in the chaos the band

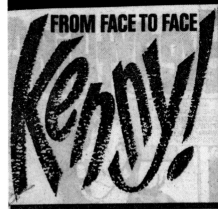

FROM FACE TO FACE

Kenny!

by DICK TATHAM

KENNY JONES

KENNY JONES will tell you he made his start in showbiz on biscuit tin !

This came about in the days of skiffle—some 11 years ago. He was eight at the time. He and some schoolmates used to go to his house to play skiffle—and biscuit-tinner was the role which came his way.

He didn't mind. Rhythm was in his blood. His idol was Brian Bennett of The Shadows.

Stepney—in East London—was Kenny's home area. He wasn't all that keen on deeper school subjects—but was a hundred per cent keen and expert when it came to woodwork and metalwork. A steady flow of useful articles in the home—bookends, coffee tables, ashtrays and so on—would be brought by him to his folks.

But the Big Idea in his life was to own a drumkit. Often of an evening he would bike to the West End and look longingly into the windows of music shops.

Kenny and Plonk Lane were the first of the Faces to get together—but their first meeting was long before the group started. Both were in different units of the Army Cadets.

" We came face to face very briefly," Kenny recalls, " when I found myself on the wrong end of a rifle held by Plonk ! "

How—some years later—their first musical meeting came about was that Kenny (just for kicks) had started playing in an East End pub. Behind the bar worked Plonk's brother Stan.

When Stan heard Plonk was looking for a drummer, he said : " I know just the bloke."

Plonk came to listen—was impressed—and it was only when they had been talking about music and other matters for some time that they realised they had met while in the cadets.

Around this time, Kenny had been saving like mad to get the £10 deposit or his first full drumkit—getting money by washing down cars after school and at weekends. His mum helped him a bit towards it.

" But," Kenny recalls, " my dad had said he was against me lashing out a lot on drums before I started earning respectable money from showbiz. I hoped to get them without him knowing. Then I realised he would have to sign the HP form as guarantor !

" But he was very kind about it when I

told him the position. He signed the form and wished me luck."

As the Faces made a name, so did Kenny build a reputation in the biz as a first-class skinsman. The other Faces also became quickly aware of how fanatical he was about his drumming.

He will practise like mad even when the group has a day off. If there are no drums handy, he will tap out time with a ruler on a desk, a knife on a table or with anything else that happens to be handy.

" We learned long ago," says Plonk, " to hide away all loose objects when Kenny is due. Otherwise he is liable to tap-tap-tap away for anything up to three hours."

To get Kenny to talk about himself is not easy. He has always been reckoned to be

" the quiet Face." He himself has said :

"When the interviews are going on with the group, I try to remain in the background and leave the questions to the other three. You could say I'm a born listener."

Just the same, there is a reasonable amount to be told about Kenny as a person.

For a long time, for example, he was the only Face with a car. (Steve Marriott is now on the point of buying one.) In April 1966—after buying a Mini with a black-and-white check bonnet—he said :

" I get a wonderful sense of freedom—driving around. I never want to go on another bus as long as I live."

More recently, Kenny has bought a beige MG.

What fascinates Kenny as much as driving a car is riding a horse. The one in question is Pedro Jones.

Kenny bought him for £240 in August last year. Pedro is kept in Essex—handy for Kenny's fave riding place, Epping Forest. (Kenny often lets Steve ride Pedro. When they go North, Steve returns the compliment with his horse—kept near Oldham.)

On his 18th birthday, Kenny registered instant delight when the other Faces gave him a super saddle for Pedro.

Not so instant was the delight he had shown over their gift on his 17th birthday. Then they stopped the van on a long night journey—Plonk saying they had a flat tyre. Steve then said he had found a parcel which looked as if it contained a human arm.

The others talked Kenny into opening it. He was dead nervy—but he did.

It contained a new foot pedal for his drumkit !

Kenny doesn't drink alcohol. He smokes only a little. He is a keen chess player. He has tried his hand at archery now and then. He is learning guitar. He eats about two pounds of fruit a day.

He has a vast disc library—containing all kinds of music, but R & B above all. He likes having a meal in his dressing gown—but admits he has never had the nerve to go to a restaurant wearing one !

Naturally, he is elated by the success the Faces have achieved.

" Success," he says, " gives you self-confidence not just as a performer—but as a person."

But he and the others have never let self-confidence turn into self-importance.

" We have always been shy," he declares, " about introducing ourselves to stars we haven't met. We don't want to be thought flash."

Vivid among Kenny's memories of the group's rise to success is the help given them early on by Sonny and Cher—and the lady of 60 who was one of their first fans.

" We met her in Sheffield," says Kenny. " She knew all the James Brown numbers we played—and kept asking if we had any more in reserve."

Taking it easy !

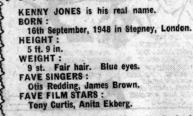

KENNY JONES is his real name.
BORN :
    16th September, 1948 in Stepney, London.
HEIGHT :
    5 ft. 9 in.
WEIGHT :
    9 st. Fair hair. Blue eyes.
FAVE SINGERS :
    Otis Redding, James Brown.
FAVE FILM STARS :
    Tony Curtis, Anita Ekberg.

FAVE COLOUR :
    Blue.
FAVE FOOD :
    Indian.
FAVE DRINK :
    Coke.
LIKES :
    Cars, horse riding, listening for new sounds.
HATES :
    Being with someone when neither knows what to say.

Valentine magazine, 1967.

87

were causing, ringing up the press and presenting them with lurid headlines such as WOULD YOU LET YOUR DAUGHTER MARRY A ROLLING STONE?

Eventually, in 1967, Allen Klein took over the Stones' business affairs, leaving Oldham to indulge in his more imaginative flights of fancy: he discovered

Rest for the practitioners of the whopping laugh.

a young Marianne Faithfull and put her together with the Stones, and in 1965, under the motto 'Happy To Be A Part Of The Industry Of Human Happiness', he launched Immediate Records. The inspiration for this had come from the States where independent labels had been established for some time. They provided Oldham with the framework with which to launch Immediate.

His first record was The McCoys' 'Hang On Sloopy', which went top ten. He followed this in 1966 with Chris Farlowe's 'Out Of Time'. It soon became apparent that the company was totally unlike the monolithic Decca or EMI labels. It was not run by ageing men who had no understanding of pop music, but staffed by young creative people constantly on the look out for new ideas and angles. From that point of view The Small Faces benefited enormously from the association. Yet their first

'I consider myself very lucky to be in the position I'm in because it's given me time to step out of the rush and see how stupid it is, because we don't live the normal life.'

RONNIE LANE, JANUARY 1967

single under new management, 'I Can't Make It'/'Just Passing' was not, thanks to the continuing contract wrangles, a success. Released by Decca on 3 March 1967, the single was a blatant attempt by the record company to cash in before the group officially departed.

'We originally signed to Don Arden whose company was Contemporary Music,' Kenney Jones explains, 'and he in turn got an arrangement with Decca whereby he held sole rights to the band, not Decca. So that's how he was able to sell us off. When he sold us on, Decca had no hold on us and Immediate were going to do the same deal, but where it all started going wrong was when our lawyer looked at the contracts.

'It all came to light that everything was illegal because when we had signed to Contemporary Music in the first place, we were all under age. So he really didn't own us at all. After Tito Burns had bought us and was selling us off again, it was still illegal. We shouldn't have been sold to him in the first place because we had never had parental signatures making it legal. Steve told Andrew what was going on and he sorted it out and bought us outright, the whole package.'

'That was a bad time for us,' said Marriott. 'I remember "I Can't Make It" came out about number twenty-six or something and I thought, "Oh great, it's going to be a hit." But because Decca had all but dropped us, dropped the option, of course the next week it had gone out. We were without a label for a few weeks, floating. It was all because we were negotiating with Andrew who wasn't flavour of the month with Decca.'

'The point is at that time we had no manager, and no one to hustle for us to get plugs. All the plugs were on London and the BBC banned it, so not many people knew it was out. It was chaos, chaos, chaos.'

STEVE MARRIOTT ON THE CHART FAILURE OF
'I CAN'T MAKE IT', APRIL 1967

Perhaps the other persuasive reason for the single's disappearance was the BBC. In their wisdom they had decided that the song's lyrics had lurid

FROM FACE TO FACE

PLONK LANE

All four famous Small Faces are known very well by the fans. Each is a personality. So it is a job to know whom to write about first.

But my choice falls on Plonk Lane—for Plonk was the one who started the Faces. How did this happen?

Well let's go back to the beginning and run over the main events in Plonk's life which eventually led up to him getting the group going . . .

PLONK was born in London's East End not quite 21 years ago. He remembers that from the age of about six he felt the urge to entertain people—singing numbers he had heard in cowboy films and banging away at a toy ukelele his folks had given him.

He also remembers that at school he wasn't all that wild about lessons—except possibly for those on drawing, at which he was very good. His final education was at Lister Technical College, in the East End.

" I left at 16," Plonk recalls. " But before then I had already made a start with earning a living. I got a job at Battersea Fun Fair during the holidays. I began on the roll-a-penny stall and worked my way up to the Big Dipper ! "

Plonk's first full-time job was assistant in a gents' outfitters.

" I would have been bored stiff with life," he says, " except for the fact I was running a group in the evenings. It was called the Outcasts."

The Outcasts played mainly to local pub 'n' club audiences. Their style was strongly influenced by the Shadows.

Plonk showed a lot more zeal for the group than for his shop job—which he left to try his hand at making deliveries (usually sets of false teeth !) for a London dental firm. This meant riding around on a scooter—hoping he wouldn't fall off too often !

Next day job : a pipe fitter's mate. The pipe fitter worked for a central heating firm. Plonk recalls that half his life seemed to be taking up floorboards—and putting 'em back once the pipes were installed.

" It is amazing," says Plonk, " the things you find under floorboards. Coins, ballpens, old razor blades, combs, buttons, keys, picture postcards—you name it, I've found it."

To his delight, Plonk then landed a day job that had to do with music. It was for a music instrument firm : assembling amplifiers.

It was during this work that he became fascinated by the sound of a bass guitar—and

BY DICK TATHAM

this was to prove a key development in the launching of the Small Faces.

For some time, Plonk had been thinking of re-fashioning his group. He had been playing lead guitar. Now he decided to switch to bass.

He went into a music shop in East Ham to trade in his guitar and buy a bass—and that was how Plonk first met Steve Marriott. Steve, you see, was working behind the counter !

It wasn't just a question of Plonk doing the deal for the bass with Steve. They also started talking about music.

Plonk already had a drummer : Kenny Jones. He asked Steve to join the group—and Steve was only too pleased. (The Small Faces—as we shall see later in this series — were completed by Jimmy Winston, who later left and was replaced by Ian McLagan).

As all good fans of the Faces know, the group's first disc—released on Decca—was *Wotcha Gonna Do About It ?* It was released in August 1965.

It must have been a worrying wait for all the group—but specially so for Plonk, as founder of the Faces. But the disc became a triumphant Number One and the Faces were well and truly on the pop scene.

But the feeling of elation over the first disc was to be followed—at the end of 1965—with a bad attack of the blues over their second.

It was called *I've Got Mine.* It failed to make the Top 20. What made this doubly disappointing was that Plonk had written it in partnership with Steve.

" We had been very bucked by our ability to dream up songs," Plonk recalls. " But our disappointment over *I've Got Mine* lasted only for a while. We figured that you don't get far in showbiz—or in any other walk of life—without being pretty determined. So we just hoped for better luck next time."

Their next disc song came from other writers : Kenny Lynch and Mort Shuman. (It was *Sha-La-La-La-Lee* —another Number One hit.)

But then Plonk teamed again with Steve to write *Hey Girl !* Results were certainly encouraging : it reached No. 12 in the charts.

Then—in the summer of 1966—Plonk and Steve came up with *All Or Nothing.* It gave them the Number One writing success for which they had hoped for so many months.

They followed through before the end of 1966 with another Top Tenner : *My Mind's Eye.*

Now let's look at Plonk behind the scenes . . . he likes experimenting with electronic sounds and would like one day to have his own workshop. He is an entertaining talker and a keen practical joker. He likes drawing cartoons—particularly of a character he has invented : Albert Frigg.

He thinks the world of his folks—phoning them each day from wherever he may be. He loves fishing—has a load of tackle—but is so busy with his career, he finds little time to drop that line.

Why the nickname Plonk ? He says :

" That's what I used to do when I first played guitar—plonk ! "

Real name : **Ronald Frederick Lane.**

Born : **Plaistow, East London, 1st April, 1946.**

Height : **5 ft. 5 in.** Weight : **8 st. 8 lb.** Hazel eyes. Dark brown hair.

Fave food : **Shepherd's pie.** Fave drink : **Coke.**

Fave artists : **Spencer Davis, Hollies.**

Likes : **Sheffield fans (" gave us first rave reception ").**

Dislikes : **Going short on sleep.**

Valentine magazine, 1967.

sexual overtones from which their audience had to be protected. Accordingly the single received no radio play or exposure. Decca then tried to repromote the B-side, a short bizarre song appropriately entitled 'Just Passing'. Which it did.

In March, the band finally signed to their manager's label and took to the road, in tow with Roy Orbison and Paul and Barry Ryan.

'The tour,' Marriott stated, 'was a right cock-up from the start. Every night we had the beehived barnet brigade sitting on one side of the theatre and all these Mods on the other. A complete divide. That was Davidson's management – he had already booked us on it and we couldn't get out of it. The last straw was Paul and Barry Ryan – *Paul and bleedin' Barry Ryan!* They were on every fucking tour

'We opened up with "Paperback Writer" the other day and then we got stuck on this riff while we listened to the electronic tape sounds. It was too much. We all got hung up listening to the tape and just backing it – but I doubt if it got through to the kids.'

STEVE MARRIOTT, AUTUMN 1967

we did because Harold Davidson was married to Marianne Ryan, so she would bring them along and he would bung them on tour. Here they come, Marianne's kids. We were going nuts. One night we nicked Roy Orbison's guitar and took it up a ton in tuning. All his songs, "Only The Lonely" and "In Dreams", were so high anyway, we thought, that'll do him. He comes on and did fine. Didn't miss a note. He knew what we'd done, knew it was us. He looked over at us all standing in the wings waiting for the fuck-up and called us cunts.'

The tour, much to the band's relief, ended on 9 April at the ABC in Romford. In May, they played the *NME* Poll Winners' concert at Wembley, along with Cat Stevens, Georgie Fame and Cream, before flying to Italy and then Scandinavia for a four-date tour.

On their return, fresh headaches awaited them. Without any notice or authorisation, Decca had announced the release on 26 May of another Small Faces single, 'Patterns'/'E Too D'.

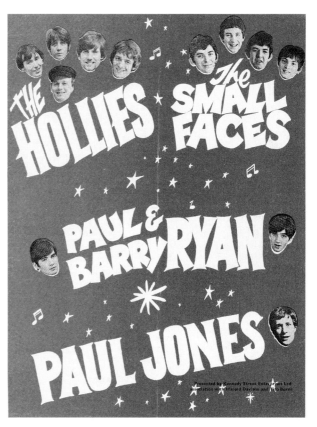

On the road with 'Paul and bleedin' Barry Ryan!'

The group were furious and refused to promote the record in any way, shape or form. They publicly asked that their fans not buy the single (they didn't and it failed to chart), and then announced the release, on 2 June, of their debut single for Immediate, 'Here Come The Nice'/'Talk To You'.

Decca responded by stating that they were about to release a second Small Faces album. Sure enough, as 'Here Come The Nice' climbed to number twelve and the group toured Holland, a hotchpotch collection of early material, demos and hit singles, entitled *From The Beginning*, was released.

Immediate swiftly hit back by rush-releasing their first album from the group, *Small Faces*. So by the end of June, The Small Faces had two albums in the racks, both in the top twenty. Furthermore, a battle of the adverts between the two record companies ensued.

On 10 June, Immediate had taken out half-page ads in all the music papers to promote 'Here Come The Nice'. To further its cause, on 13 June the band performed the single on the enormously popular

BBC show *Dee Time*. Unlike its Decca rival, the record sold well.

Not to be outdone, Decca, a week after the Immediate adverts, splashed out on equal ad space to promote *From The Beginning*. The tag-line was 'The Small Faces At Their Best'. The next week readers were further bemused to be presented with yet another Immediate advert which boldly stated, 'Whichever Way You Look At It, There Are Only Four Small Faces But There Is Just One Small Faces LP And It's On Immediate'.

Two weeks later, with the Decca album stalling at number seventeen in the charts and its Immediate rival staring down on it from four places above, Andrew Loog Oldham declared his company the winner.

Artistically, the Immediate camp had also scored a direct hit. The LP contained fourteen tracks, all of which came in in under three minutes. Eleven of the songs were written by Marriott and Lane with McLagan contributing one song, 'Up The Wooden Hills To Bedfordshire', and receiving a co-writing credit on 'Eddie's Dreaming'. The superb 'Green Circles' was written with Michael O'Sullivan, the band's live-in chauffeur at Pimlico.

This varied but artistically consistent work, as evidenced through songs such as 'Get Yourself Together', 'Talk To You', 'Something I Want To Tell You' and 'Things Are Going To Get Better', fully served to confirm the enormous versatility and strength of the songwriting team and their supporting cast.

'I'm sure they wrote separately and together,' Glyn Johns states. 'I wasn't there when they wrote but I don't remember a lot of songs being started on a session. I think one might come in with an idea and it would be built on from there. But sometimes they would come in with an entire song.'

According to Ronnie Lane, by this time the pair had gained enough experience and confidence to write on their own, although their songs were always credited to Marriott and Lane, except, of course, those songs to which Jones and McLagan had contributed.

... whichever way you look at it, there are only four Small Faces. But there is just one Small Faces LP Its on IMMEDIATE IMLP/SPOO8·

The battle of the ads between Immediate and Decca begins.

FROM FACE TO FACE Mac!

KEY day in the life of Ian McLagan was 1st November, 1965—for that was when he became one of the Small Faces.

It was a turn of events which would have excited him at the best of times. As it happened, it gave him an extra-special excitement because just before the offer came, all had not been well with his career.

Let us now take up the story of Ian—going first into how he came to receive the offer from the Faces—and then into what happened after he had eagerly accepted it . . .

Unlike the other Faces, Ian (or Mac as the others call him) was not brought up in the East End of London. He was born in Hounslow, Middlesex, almost 21 years ago.

His dad was Scots, his mum Irish. He took an interest in playing piano when only seven. His mum bought an old upright and—with blocks on the pedals to enable him to reach them—he began to tinkle out tunes.

"I must confess," he says today, "that the novelty wore off after a while. I would probably have packed up, except that Mum kept on at me. It's a good thing she did otherwise I might never have got into showbiz."

Mac went to the Spring Grove Grammar School in Isleworth, Middlesex. He was interested enough in music to join a school group called the Blue Men, which specialised in Lonnie Donegan favourites like *Rock Island Line*.

When Mac left grammar school, he went on to Twickenham Art College to study commercial design. Also—in his spare time—he began to take piano lessons from a lady near London Airport, not far away.

"But," he says today, "there was the big snag that I was going through a mad craze for snooker. Often, when I should have been at a piano lesson, I was at the local saloon practising shots for all I was worth."

At 16, he joined a local group called the Muleskinners. When he left college, he made do with a succession of part-time jobs—trying for all he was worth to establish himself full-time in showbiz.

In this attempt, he switched to a group called the Boz People, backing solo singer, Boz.

"But," recalls Mac, "things didn't work out as I had hoped. I was doing a fantastic amount of travelling. I wouldn't have minded that, except I wasn't earning the vast sums of money I had always dreamed of earning from showbiz.

"I was in such a blue mood, I was thinking of packing up the business and taking an ordinary job. Then came that all-important call from the Small Faces, asking me to step in as Jimmy Winston was leaving.

"I learned later that they had heard me with the Boz People and thought I was okay for them. As for me, I knew all about the Small Faces.

"It gave a wonderful boost to my morale to think they wanted me with them. The great thing was that—quite apart from the music—I seemed to fit in as regards appearance.

"When I got together with Plonk, Kenny and Steve, it was like meeting my brothers !"

Mac confesses that when he first appeared with the group, he was scared in case the fans gave him the bird. But the other Faces have said often that the reason they wanted Mac was that—apart from being the right size—he was a first-rate organist.

The fans agreed—and gave him a big welcome. His first disc with the Faces was *Sha-La-La-La-Lee*. It was issued in January, 1966 and was a smash hit.

Mac felt proud to have played his part in it. He has been playing a key part in the success story of the Faces ever since

What is Mac like ?

Well, he is often looked on as "the quiet Face." At group interviews, he usually leaves most of the talking to the others.

IAN McLAGAN

But once you have broken the ice with him, he will chat away in a lively, intelligent style. He is dead keen on sport of all kinds. He recalls that at school his favourite subjects were sport and maths and that he hated history.

As regards clothes, he says. his tastes are mainly modern, but that he has moments when he likes to dress conservatively. For casual wear, he is mad about bright-coloured shirts with an open weave.

Mac has many happy memories of the days when the Faces shared a big house in Pimlico, London.

"It was great," he said, "because we were all so keen on discussing either music or any other subject which happened to come up. We would sit up all night talking on occasions."

Though Mac's fave instrument is organ, he is also a skilled guitarist. He says he learned a lot about guitar by listening to the discs of one of his idols, Chuck Berry.

More Facts on Mac
IAN McLAGAN is his real name.
BORN : Hounslow, Middlesex, 12th May, 1946.
HEIGHT : 5 ft. 5 ins.
WEIGHT : 8 st. 2 lb. Dark-brown hair. Green eyes.
FAVE FOOD : Fresh fruit.
FAVE DRINK : Coke.
FAVE ARTISTS : Georgie Fame, Alan Price.
LIKES : Tenpin bowling, model car racing.
DISLIKES : "Doorstep" sandwiches in transport cafés.

Mac plays everything by ear. But he confesses he would like one day to learn to read music.

"I wish now," he says, "that I had stayed with my piano lessons properly years ago. Trouble is that when you are with a group that is doing at all well, there is so much work and travelling, you have little time for other things."

As a long-term ambition, Mac says he would like to buy a small island in the South Seas one day where he could be "away from it all" for weeks on end.

If he does, I bet there will be fans turning up there somehow !

By DICK TATHAM

Valentine magazine, 1967.

Certainly, this first Immediate album not only displayed a leap forward in terms of the band's strong identity, but also illustrated their mastery at production.

By contrast, the Decca album, which also contained 'My Way Of Giving' and 'Tell Me Have You Ever Seen Me', presented three covers: Del Shannon's 'Runaway' (which features Don Arden on backing vocals), Marvin Gaye's 'Baby Don't Do It' and Smokey Robinson's 'You Really Got A Hold On Me', plus several past hits, 'All Or Nothing', 'My Mind's Eye', 'Hey Girl', 'Sha La La La Lee' and 'What'cha Gonna Do About It'. The rest was work that had been written but discarded by the band in favour of other material.

Oldham's claims of victory were therefore justified. Meanwhile, 'Here Come The Nice', one of the greatest tributes to amphetamines known to pop, gave the band sweet and proper revenge over the stuffy BBC censors. Somehow the guardians of public morality had managed to miss completely lines such as, 'He knows what I want/He's got what I need/He's always there/When I need some speed'.

'Nice' mixes soft, slightly psychedelic verses with a rousing chorus, the melody of which could have come straight off an authentic Stax horn riff. The same applied to much of their debut Immediate album – it was psychedelic soul/pop of the highest order.

On the personal front, however, there had been some changes – the group had now moved out of their Pimlico house. The lease had come up for renewal, and with the neighbours constantly complaining about noise and the fans who congregated there, the band were forced to take their own separate abodes.

After only three weeks, Steve is ejected from a flat in Kensington – his third move in a few months.

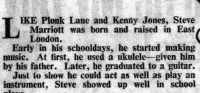

FACE TO FACE Steve!

STEVE MARRIOTT

By **DICK TATHAM**

L IKE Plonk Lane and Kenny Jones, Steve Marriott was born and raised in East London.

Early in his schooldays, he started making music. At first, he used a ukulele—given him by his father. Later, he graduated to a guitar.

Just to show he could act as well as play an instrument, Steve showed up well in school plays.

Steve earned his break into paid showbiz when only 12. His father took him to an audition for the West End production of *Oliver !*

The young hopeful landed a part—and played it successfully for a year. Then he had to leave for the same reason as some of the other lads : he was starting to look too old !

Just the same, he had the satisfaction of singing the part of the Artful Dodger on an L.P. of the show.

Naturally, Steve couldn't give his whole efforts to show business. Rightly, he spent a lot of time on his basic education.

But his acting ability was beginning to attract more and more attention. He landed a part in a children's film serial. He appeared on TV in episodes of *Citizen James, Mr. Pastry* and *Dixon of Dock Green.* He also landed a part in the Peter Sellers film, *Heavens Above.*

And in the meantime, he had made a start on disc . . .

His disc debut really started through his songs.

He had for some time been trying his hand at composing songs. He felt that one of them—*Imaginary Love*—had possibilities. Steve—then 15 years old —tried to interest publishers in Tin Pan Alley.

But he had no luck. Then he thought of his Aunt Sheila. She was secretary to the late Jack Hylton, one of Britain's big showbusiness bosses. He phoned and asked her help.

She spoke to Mr. Hylton. He gave Steve an intro to a music publisher (who, as it happened, was not in Tin Pan Alley !)

The music publisher liked the song. But he liked Steve's voice even better.

He arranged an audition with Decca. They issued a disc of Steve singing *Give Her My Regards.* It didn't make the charts.

"But," Steve recalls, "I reckoned it was good experience and that I was still young enough to hope for another chance on disc."

As we know today, that came through his membership of the Small Faces.

As to how he came to join the group—well, Steve had to take a succession of ordinary jobs to fill in the gaps between showbiz ones.

One job was "ordinary" with a touch of showbiz. It was working in a music shop in East Ham, London.

"One day," Steve told me when I talked to him recently, "a chap came in with a guitar that had seen better days. He wanted to trade it in for a new bass guitar. We fixed a deal— and got talking about music in general.

"This bloke told me his name was Plonk Lane—and that he was re-forming the group he was running locally. When I said I could sing a bit and play guitar, he said was I interested ? I most certainly was.

"Soon I was a member of The Small Faces."

Today The Small Faces are established as top pop stars. They have a long list of successes to their credit.

But in their early days—after they had taken the gamble of becoming fulltime professionals— it was tough. Steve particularly recalls their experience when they went to a date in Sheffield —for only £5 a man.

"We happened to find ourselves faced with an audience of mainly middle-aged people," he told me. " Our stuff just wasn't right for them. We were paid off after three numbers. We walked through the local streets feeling utterly brought down.

"Then we came to the entrance to a club that looked bright and with-it. We could see lots of young people going in. On the spur of the moment, we went in and told the owner we would play for nothing.

"He agreed. We played for all we were worth, taking courage from the fact that the audience were mainly teenagers. Well, we went a bomb.

"The audience raved like mad and kept yelling for more. Though we had told the owner we didn't want anything, he gave us a fiver towards our expenses. So we went back to London happy.

"Or, at least, we started out happy. What took the edge off things was that we ran out of petrol on the way back and had to wait for a filling station to open."

In the success story of The Small Faces— which started with their chart-hitting *Whatcha Gonna Do About It* in the summer of 1965, Steve has played a prominent role both as a performer and (in partnership with Plonk) a songwriter.

He says he loves all the travelling he has done with the group. He is trying all the time to develop as a musician, currently being able to play ukulele, guitar, drums, organ and harmonica.

He is also a keen horse rider, liking nothing better than to relax from show business by taking a canter through the countryside. Also, he has by no means lost his interest in acting . . . a very important interest in his life as it happens.

"I am still only 20," he says. " That gives me plenty of time to let my pop career run its course—and after that to concentrate on an acting career."

Latest hit by The Small Faces—*I Can't Make It*— involved more success for Steve.

He sang lead vocal. He wrote the song with Plonk Lane and they also penned the B side : *Just Passing.*

Steve and Plonk also pro- duced the session at which the disc was made. They are also starting to produce discs by other performers.

It all adds up to : Small Faces—Big Talent !

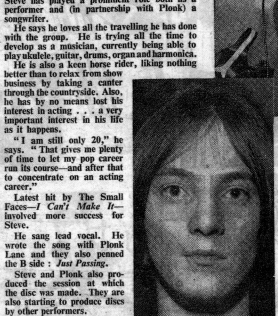

MORE FACTS ON STEVE

STEVE MARRIOTT is his real name.
BORN 30th January, 1947 in Stepney, London,
HEIGHT : 5 ft. 4 in.
WEIGHT : Eight stone. Brown hair. Green eyes.
FAVE SINGERS : Ray Charles, James Brown.
FAVE FILM STARS : Ursula Andress, Peter Sellers.
FAVE FOOD AND DRINK : Steak and salad, vintage cider.
LIKES : Riding, antique shops.
DISLIKES : " In " clubs.

Valentine magazine, 1967.

'We moved out last week. The lease ran out and we didn't think it was worth renewing again, so we've all got pads of our own. A change of scene. I've moved into a new pad and it seems as if I've lived there all my life. But the one in Pimlico . . . we were there for a year and it was a drag leaving it, we had so many scenes there.'

RONNIE LANE, FEBRUARY 1967

'That one year at the Pimlico place has been a complete mindblaster for me. We used to sit around and talk for hours and hours – and this is what people couldn't understand, because we'd sooner talk than go out. We'd make arrangements to go out to a club or something and then one of us would begin a discussion and it would go on until four in the morning. Everybody helped everybody else – and if I hadn't been in that atmosphere I wouldn't have had a fantastic realisation of everything.'

RONNIE LANE, FEBRUARY 1967

Marriott, as ever, could not keep still. Thanks to his predilection for noise, he had no sooner moved into a new flat when the complaints came in thick and fast and, once again, he was forced out.

'I've got to move out of the flat this week. It'll be the third time this year. Cilla Black lives underneath and you'd think she would understand but she has been complaining the most. I'm sorry I make so much noise but I'm only having fun and they all complain. What a drag. Isn't there anyone who digs a few sounds?'

STEVE MARRIOTT ON BEING ASKED TO QUIT HIS
BAKER STREET PAD, APRIL 1967

In July, news of an old Small Faces member, Jimmy Winston, came through. After leaving the group, Winston had recorded a single for Decca, 'Sorry She's Mine'/'It's Not What You Do'. It had gone nowhere. Now signed to RCA, his new group, Winston Fumbs, had just released their debut 45 entitled 'Real Crazy Apartment.' The single stalled and the one-time organist was not heard of again until he was spotted, baring all, in the stage production of *Hair*. He made a couple more singles for

NEMS in the seventies and now runs a musical equipment business.

On 5 August, the group were beneficiaries of a typically imaginative Immediate-inspired ad campaign. Half of that week's *NME* cover was taken up with a picture of four little boys in the countryside holding up a road sign that read 'Itchycoo Park'. Readers had to turn to the review section to discover that the mysterious ad was announcing the release of the band's tenth single.

'It's been a strange disc. I don't want to sound conceited but it was the only one of our records which I personally felt would go to number one.'

IAN McLAGAN, AUTUMN 1967

'Itchycoo Park'/'I'm Only Dreaming' is a groundbreaking single, thanks to an effect known as phasing, which is judiciously used throughout the track. Phasing is the technique of distorting a certain instrument by means of echoing and lengthening its recorded sound. According to Glyn Johns, the man responsible for this technical breakthrough, George Chiantz, has never been fully credited for his role.

Marriott tuning up.

SCOTT McKENZIE ▶ AMAZING FLOWER REVELATIONS

TOP POP NEWS

• TOM JONES
• LULU • TAMLA • LOVE-IN
• TAILPIECES — POPLAND'S TOP COLUMN

New Musical Express

EVERY FRIDAY 6D

No. 1073   Week ending August 5th, 1967
WORLD'S LARGEST CIRCULATION OF ANY MUSIC PAPER

DAVY'S FRANK CONFESSION

BIG SMASH HIT!
SANDIE SHAW's
GREAT FOLLOW-UP TO "PUPPET ON A STRING"
TONIGHT IN TOKYO
on PYE CERISE 7N 17346
K.P.M., 21 DENMARK STREET, W.C.2   TEM 3856

HOME!

from their Greek holiday on Monday came JOHN LENNON, PAUL McCARTNEY and his girl friend, actress JANE ASHER—all looking very relaxed, to be greeted by the happy news of Mick and Keith.

FREE!

from the shadow of prison which has hung over the young lives of MICK JAGGER and KEITH RICHARD for five weeks. The appeal court gave Mick a conditional discharge, which meant he will not serve his three month sentence, and Keith had his conviction quashed due to the original judge erring in not instructing the jury on all the points.

And now back to the STONES as musicians and their next single   **DON'T MISS IT**

A 4-PAGE SPECIAL SUPPLEMENT IN NEXT WEEK'S NME!

97

Sideburns and a bass: Lane on TV.

'It was nothing to do with The Small Faces at all,' he asserts. 'I turned up for the session that we cut "Itchycoo Park" and my assistant on that date was a guy called George Chiantz who was an extremely bright fellow.

'He was very technically minded and he figured out how to use phasing by using three tape machines. When I arrived he said, "Look what I've worked out this morning, I've finally managed to make it work," and he showed me what he had done. I thought it was absolutely fantastic. The band arrived for the session and we cut "Itchycoo Park" Then I said, "You know what we should do? I've got to show you this," and that's how it came about. I can't take any credit for it. It was George Chiantz. He came up with the idea.'

The East End site that inspired the lyrics was to be located in three-quarters of the group's collective childhood memories.

'It's a place we used to go to in Ilford years ago. Some bloke we know suggested it to us because it's full of nettles and you keep scratching.'
RONNIE LANE ON THE TRUE LOCATION OF ITCHYCOO PARK, AUTUMN 1967

'Itchycoo Park,' Jones recalls, 'wasn't really a park, it was an area in Ilford which was a bombsite, an area of wasteland all wild and overgrown that ran down to the railway lines, which was full of stinging nettles [hence the title the locals bestowed on the area]. The record came in bits and pieces and Glyn Johns did much to pull it together. He didn't produce it, he was engineer, but he had lots of ideas. Whether we listened to him or not was another matter.

'We had the idea of introducing phasing which was a new thing then. It's a continuous tape loop of sound played over and over but it was all new then. I remember something happened to one of the tape reels. It was broken so we set up one reel and looped it round a chair leg at the other end so it could still run continuously. And that was phasing.'

To promote the single the band undertook the normal round of promotional interviews. One of these was a live radio appearance by Marriott.

'I did this pop quiz on the radio,' Marriott recalled, 'for Ray Moore the DJ and one of the questions was, "How did you get the effects on 'Itchycoo Park'?" It was a live audience and I said, "I pissed on the tape," and his face! Well, if looks could kill. Nobody laughed, there's just dead silence. It was simple. Just one tape repeated, one tape against the other. But I couldn't tell them all that. It's boring. There wasn't a sound in the studio and I'm laughing me head off until I realised I was the only one.'

'Itchycoo Park', which reached number three in the UK, was also notable as the band's one and only chart hit in the States, rising to number sixteen.

'It was this really beautiful day and we were doing some dates in Norway last month. We were standing by this lake and Pat Arnold said something to Ronnie that just brought the idea back. So we wrote the song while we were there.'

STEVE MARRIOTT ON WRITING
'ITCHYCOO PARK', AUTUMN 1967

The genesis of the song had begun in a hotel room. Lane had read the hotel leaflet extolling the virtues of Oxford with its 'dreamy spires'. He wrote the first verse and the beginning of another before showing it to Marriott who obliged with the song's middle eight. Then, together, they finished the song that many consider to be one of their classics. In truth, it furthered the belief that the group could only produce gimmicky songs that dealt with their childhood experiences.

In mid-August, Kenney announced his engagement to actress Jan Osborne (they would marry three years later). Marriott, who was besotted with a model called Jenny Rylands, was busy writing a song to try to persuade her of his charms. Ronnie Lane was seeing a singer by the name of Geneveve, and McLagan was keeping quiet about his relationship with TV dancer Sandy Sargent.

A week after the announcement of Kenney's engagement the group played the Festival of Flower Children at Woburn Abbey, where they headlined the Saturday night bill above Eric Burdon, Jeff Beck

On tour in Copenhagen, circa 1967.

and The Bee Gees. Unfortunately, as the audience had been handed free sparklers, a nearby canopy caught fire and the band's performance was cut short.

At the end of the month, as a sign of their huge popularity in Germany, the group were invited to appear on the country's first ever TV colour transmission in a live concert that also featured their fellow Immediate artists Twice As Much and singer P. P. Arnold.

A former Ikette with Ike and Tina Turner, Arnold had arrived in Britain for a tour and been introduced to Mick Jagger by Glyn Johns. He persuaded her to stay in London. Soon after, she signed to Immediate where she met The Small Faces and invited them to write something for her. Marriott played her the song he had been writing for Jenny Rylands, a new number entitled 'Tin Soldier'. On hearing the tune in rough form, Arnold's reaction was so enthusiastic it gave the songwriter second thoughts.

'The meaning of the song ["Tin Soldier"] is about getting into somebody's mind – not their body. It refers to a girl I used to talk to all the time and she really gave me a buzz. The single was to give her a buzz in return and maybe other people as well. I dig it. There's no great message really and no physical scenes.'

STEVE MARRIOTT, DECEMBER 1967

'We played it for Pat Arnold,' Marriott recalled, 'and she freaked over it so much I thought, I'd better hold back! It was just too good to let go. We later wrote her one called "If You Think You're Groovy".'

Another Immediate artist to benefit from Marriott and Lane's creativity was singer Billy Nicholls. Just after leaving school, he had been signed to Immediate as a teen songwriter but soon began cutting his own material.

Marriott and Lane gave him one of their discarded songs, 'Would You Believe', and produced the track themselves. The single appeared the next year backed by Nicholls's own 'Day Time Girl'. Along with pianist Nicky Hopkins and John Paul Jones, The

Small Faces then played and helped produce Nicholls's debut album, also entitled Would You Believe. It was released in 1968 but in such small quantities that it quickly disappeared. (In 1974, the GM label gave the album a 'proper' release. Today, it currently has an asking price of £150.)

That month, August, also saw Marriott guesting on the Stones album, Their Satanic Majesties Request. He played guitar and sang backing vocals on one of the LP's better tracks, 'In Another Land'.

'That came about due to us using the same studios,' Marriott explained. 'I'd been in there from the night before working on our own stuff and Bill Wyman came over and said, "Do you want to have a play on this?" It was simple. No arranging or complications. Everyone used to do it. If there was someone in next door that you liked, and you were coming in, you would think, what can they do on this or that?

'Brian Jones wasn't there, he was off doing his own thing, so I filled in for him. I was apparently considered as a possible replacement because Brian was on his way out, but I wouldn't have taken it. Later I talked to Keith about it but back then Mick wouldn't have it.

'I don't blame him. Keith would have liked it and I would have thought about it, because it would have been another backing vocal and a strong one. I don't think Mick took us seriously. In fact, whoever came into contact with us couldn't take us seriously, we were too busy laughing. We were always stoned and laughing so I don't see how he could have. The funny thing is that a little while later Brian rang me up and asked if he could come over and have a play, which was great. Everyone was really excited about it. He was a nice bloke when he wasn't out of it, which was most of the time. A shame because he was a great player when he was straight.'

Marriott didn't just donate his musical services to the Stones song. Months previously, during the recording of their debut Immediate album, Marriott had been struggling over some lyrics for a Latin/Calypso number. As he deliberated, he noticed that one of their roadies, Eddie, had fallen asleep in the studio and was snoring loudly.

Suitably inspired, Marriott named his song

'Eddie's Dreaming' and taped the sleeping beauty's snoring, although they were unable to use the sound in the final mix. When he helped out the Stones, Marriott gave them the tape, which the group cheekily used on 'In Another Land'.

In October, an Immediate package featuring The Small Faces, P. P. Arnold, Chris Farlowe and The Nice went on a two-week European TV and radio campaign. Part of the schedule included a day at Camber Sands to shoot a film, the second of its kind, to promote Immediate and its artists. The director was Peter Whitehead, who had already worked with the group on the promo film for 'Get Yourself Together' that had been shot at Regent's Park. The video's storyline was based on an encounter that Marriott had had with the police after leaving a club late one night. Consequently, 'Get Yourself Together' features Marriott being chased and then apprehended by the rest of the group who are all dressed as policemen. This premise is repeated ad infinitum.

For the shooting of the second Immediate film, Whitehead travelled to Camber Sands with Oldham and The Small Faces.

'We got into Andrew Loog Oldham's Rolls-Royce,' Whitehead recalled, 'and got absolutely smashed. We arrived at Camber Sands just as the sun was coming out and we were all out of our minds. Then I just held the camera and we shot a whole lot of footage.'

The filming included The Small Faces performing 'Itchycoo Park' and then backing P. P. Arnold as she rolled seductively around in the sea singing 'First Cut Is The Deepest'.

In November a one-week tour of Ireland had been pencilled in, but was scrapped when Marriott, once more suffering from nervous exhaustion, collapsed and was ordered to rest.

Ian McLagan, taking advantage of this unexpected break, decided to take his girlfriend, Sandy Sargent, on holiday. At the airport a lump of dope was discovered on him. The rest of the group found out about it later that night while watching TV.

'They were both arrested,' Jones recalls. 'It was terrible. They were both on the news and we had to get the lawyers to bail them out. It was a whole new

drug problem that wouldn't be resolved until years later after we had formed The Faces and even then we had to play some places without him.'

As both Marriott and McLagan recuperated from their respective ordeals, the band's eleventh single, 'Tin Soldier'/'Feel Much Better', was released. The A-side was a magnificent song which had no difficulty soaring to number nine in the charts, but for Marriott there was an extra bonus. Jenny Rylands had agreed to marry him (they were wed the following year).

'I'd tried every trick in the book to pull her and couldn't,' he recalled. 'So I wrote her that song and she married me!'

'Tin Soldier' was a great measure of Marriott's growing maturity as a first-class songwriter. Not only is it one of the best examples of his magnificent vocals caught in full flight but the song's arrangement flew directly against all received pop wisdom. Its series of stops, starts and various organ and guitar breaks all magically merge together to create an outstanding piece of work. Appropriately, P. P. Arnold contributed backing vocals and made various TV appearances with the band to help promote the single.

After a difficult year things, it seemed, were going to get better.

Steve with P. P. Arnold performing 'Tin Soldier'.

The band's verdict on the music business, circa 1968.

1968: OWN UP TIME

As if to emphasise the distance The Small Faces wanted to put between themselves and their teen-idol image, their look, in keeping with the times, loosened up considerably. Bouffants and button downs went out and long hair and colourful clothes came in. Heavy touring was now a thing of the past and the studio became their home from home.

The recent advances in recording technology had excited the group and they were eager to see how far they could go.

For Marriott and Co., music had become far too serious, too intellectual. The arrival of doom-laden records from the likes of Jefferson Airplane or 'The Chocolate Vanilla Underground', as Marriott once called them, had killed the spirit of fun. Even The Beatles, who had inspired this new wave of music, had ditched the colourful style of *Sgt Pepper* and were busy putting together their often brilliant but darkly meandering *White Album*.

It was fitting that pop music should assume a solemn air, for 1968 was a year filled with tragedy, the year in which Martin Luther King and Robert Kennedy were gunned down, extinguishing the torch of freedom that both men had represented. For those fighting the Establishment these were terrible blows, and the music which represented them was notably short on laughs.

If these cataclysmic events affected The Small Faces, it never showed. Their weapon against the world was humour and their refuge was the studio. If they weren't in there recording their own material, then they would willingly help out others. The group was prolific and hard-working and, in that sense, Immediate was the perfect place to be. Andrew Loog Oldham had literally thrown open the studio doors and told the band to stay as long as they liked. Any monetary considerations were to be left for Immediate to worry about. When the bills came in a year later it would prove to have been a costly decision.

'We play what we want to play. No one tells us what to play and what not to play. If people don't like our records they don't buy them. It's up to us what we record and what we don't.'

STEVE MARRIOTT, AUTUMN 1967

Left to their own devices, the group forged ahead, perfecting their unique brand of pop/soul which they tinged with psychedelia and their irresistible humour. This sound, they reasoned, would be the perfect antidote to the earnest music that had sprung up around them.

In 1968 they would create an album that contained all of these elements, *Ogdens' Nut Gone Flake*. For many people, it was the group's ultimate expression and a classic example of sixties creativity. This album would finally bring them the respect they so clearly deserved. What they didn't know was that it would also kill them off.

Four days into 1968, Ian McLagan married twenty-year-old *Ready Steady Go* dancer, Sandy Sargent. In keeping with the organist's penchant for privacy, the event was a tight secret. Not even the rest of the band knew of the ceremony, which was held at Marylebone Registry Office. They only found out later that day when McLagan joined them at the *Top Of The Pops* studio.

'I wanted to keep it secret because with the fans and everything, they get moody if you get married. After the ceremony, I dashed down to the *Top Of The Pops* studio, I can't remember what song it was, probably "Tin Soldier", but I remember Johnny Stewart, the producer, was pissed off because I was late.

'So I said to him, "Aren't you going to congratulate me? I just got married." He was all right after that and that's when the rest of the band found out.'

That month, two more Marriott/Lane songs were issued on Immediate. One was P. P. Arnold's 'If You Think You're Groovy' and the second was singer Billy Nicholls's 'Would You Believe'. The latter, with its over-the-top production, failed to chart while

Ian McLagan marries *Ready Steady Go* dancer Sandy Sargent. Not even the group knew about the occasion.

Gered Mankowitz shot taken at Ronnie Lane's flat, 1968.

Arnold's single, a glorious pop epic, spent four weeks in the charts but only reached a very disappointing forty-one.

Still, it was obvious now that Marriott and Lane had replaced Jagger and Richards as Immediate's prestigious songwriters and producers.

'The Stones were coming to the end of their relationship with Andrew,' Marriott explained. 'Ronnie and me were up there all the time working on one thing or another, so it was a gradual thing to end up filling in.'

The previous year, Marriott's connection with the

105

An artist's impression: The Small Faces, circa 1968.

Stones had taken a darkly comic turn when he ran into Marianne Faithfull again.

'Mick and Marianne Faithfull had been getting it together,' Marriott stated. 'They had had a mutual fancy on for ages . . . I'd known her before Mick. I'd been the first one to leave the house in Pimlico where we all lived. I got a little flat around the corner on my own and one night they all rang me and said, "Marianne is here looking for you." They had heard that she had a fancy on for me, which was a wind-up, but I thought, sod it, I'll have a bath and go and have a look.

'So I went round and she had been and gone. She left me a little note saying, "Come to my house." Then they said, "We'll all go with you, we'll come with you and have a laugh." Acid had just come out and it was just the thing to do at the time and it came really strong. It came in brown lysergic bottles. So we all had a bit of it on a biscuit, which was an idiot thing to do, and we all went steaming over there.

'Well, we got the right horrors as soon as we got there. There were all these moody actors and actresses wandering around in this moody atmosphere. I had gone with every intention of having a good time, which I think she did too, but when I got there she looked like the biggest ugliest tart I had ever seen in my life. The acid had hit and I just wanted to go home because all her face was moving about and she had great big jam tart lips.

'The Miracles record "Oh Baby Baby" was on and she kept sliding over to me, whispering the words to it in my ear. I was getting right paranoid and was looking for a way out and she was getting the right hump with me. Mac had locked himself in her bathroom, which had a mosaic floor, and he was well gone, banging on the door, screaming for help to get him out. [McLagan was in the bathroom, sitting down and admiring the mosaic floor. When he decided to leave he began pushing the door instead of pulling it. He panicked, convinced he was locked in a toilet for the rest of his life, and started screaming.]

'No one could hear him because the music was so loud and this floor was doing his head in,' Marriott continues. 'It was a right disaster, a sheer disaster. So I ran away from that and she got it on with Mick. I did try and explain to her before I left but you can never explain these things. It never comes out sounding right so she got the hump even more.'

On 20 January, the group, with The Who and Paul Jones in tow, left for a fifteen-day tour of Australia and New Zealand, a tour that would be marked by chaos, trouble and perhaps the first public example of what could happen if a bored Keith Moon, The Who's mercurial drummer, was left in a hotel room with time on his hands.

Prior to their departure, the battle lines had already been drawn up when one of Sydney's leading papers ran an article bemoaning the amount of money that the tour would take out of Australia.

'We was really tired,' Lane is quoted as saying in Dave Marsh's Who biography, *Before I Get Old*. 'We got off the plane, walked down the steps and there's the media waiting at the bottom of the stairs. And the first thing they said to us was, "How do you feel now that the pound's been devalued?" (The devaluation had occurred in November 1967.) As if that meant anything to us – and it was supposed to. The whole thing was so bloody and horrible and pathetic. I think Pete Townshend hit this fellow and this is what got the tour off to a good bollocking in the press.

On his twenty-first birthday, Marriott reads the bad press in the Auckland papers. Lane, as ever, can only laugh.

STEVE MARRIOTT

JANUARY 1968						
SUN	MON	TUES	WED	THURS	FRI	SAT
*	1	2	3	4	5	6
7	8	9	10	11	12	13
14	15	16	17	18	19	20
21	22	23	24	25	26	27
28	29	30	31	*	*	*

FEBRUARY 1968						
SUN	MON	TUES	WED	THURS	FRI	SAT
*	*	*	*	1	2	3
4	5	6	7	8	9	10
11	12	13	14	15	16	17
18	19	20	21	22	23	24
25	26	27	28	29	*	*

MARCH 1968						
SUN	MON	TUES	WED	THURS	FRI	SAT
*	*	*	*	*	1	2
3	4	5	6	7	8	9
10	11	12	13	14	15	16
17	18	19	20	21	22	23
24	25	26	27	28	29	30

'And then, of course, the media slagged us. They made us look so demonic that we decided in the end that we might as well go and do some of these things. We started to live up to our name, which really wasn't very satisfying, cos we really wasn't that bad.'

The press continued to tag the groups, in Marriott's words like 'dirty flee-ridden thieves', throughout the tour, which was scheduled to take them to Brisbane, Sydney, Adelaide, Melbourne, Auckland and Wellington.

On their arrival in Sydney, a press conference was held at which Marriott was asked if he smoked dope. He told his interviewer where to get off. At their gig in the Sydney Stadium, a malfunctioning revolving stage then added to their woes.

'It's my insistence on privacy that gets me a difficult reputation. If someone asks questions that are too personal I just refuse to answer them. I can get quite rude about it too. Everyone says an Englishman's home is his castle. Not any more it isn't. It's more like his rabbit hutch.'

STEVE MARRIOTT, JUNE 1968

'Many of the kids,' Marriott explained, 'only got a look at our backs because the revolving stage wouldn't revolve and naturally they were disappointed. We couldn't turn round because of our equipment and they never really saw us. I got forty geezers to push the thing round in the second house and it wouldn't move.'

At another gig, a member of the audience spent his time flicking bits of paper at Marriott as he sat playing the organ. After a few minutes, Marriott stopped playing and offered to come down and sort the guy out. The next day the papers reported that he had offered to fight the entire audience.

'All our real trouble came from these adult males with big body complexes,' Marriott reasoned. 'In Melbourne there were about six of them waiting outside the hotel and Keith Moon was with me. He doesn't frighten easily. We started breathing hard through our noses and Keith asked if anyone wanted a kicking? No one did and they ran off. But can you honestly believe that we went looking for trouble? I ask you, how could I afford to be hostile with my body?'

Further trouble ensued when the group later took a plane back to Sydney to catch a connecting flight to New Zealand. On the flight an altercation between the travelling British contingent and a disgruntled stewardess broke out.

'Everyone was dosing or sleeping at the time,' Kenney Jones recalls, 'and the stewardess started serving coffee. Bobby Pridden [Who roadie] asked for his coffee and the stewardess said, "You've already got a drink," and walked right past him. At the time you couldn't get beer served on a plane but this Australian group [Paul Jones's backing band] who were travelling with us had some and she thought everyone had their own stash, which we didn't.

'So Bobby started saying to her, "I want my coffee, where's my coffee?" and then everyone woke up and a huge row started.'

While the stewardess argued with the bands, the pilot radioed ahead. When they landed the cops were waiting for them.

'They came on the plane,' Kenney Jones recalls, 'and fumigated the whole of it with disinfectant as soon as it landed. They lined us all up on the tarmac, with our hands on our heads, and we're saying, "You can't do this, we're British." It was hilarious.'

'The stewardess started it,' Marriott recalled. 'She started on Bobby Pridden. She called him a dirty disgusting old man. All right, he might have had a few shrimps in his beard but he wasn't like that. He took a natural humbrance to it and called her a stupid cunt. So she went screaming to the captain and got the captain to take the plane down and put us all in the nick. Paul Jones was our spokesman and he's saying to the police in his best Oxford accent, "Now look here, chaps, this really isn't on," and all these hooligans are behind their backs pulling faces and making him laugh.'

The next day the news of the fracas on the plane reached the British press. Articles accusing the groups of letting down Britain's image abroad took up several column inches. What the papers failed to report was that the stewardess had been sacked, the pilot reprimanded and the groups given an apology by the chairman of the airline.

The tour moved on to New Zealand. At the first Auckland concert, Marriott stormed off stage after just three numbers. Chris Neill, a fan who was present at the show, remembers that halfway through their cover of 'Every Little Bit Hurts' Marriott had said, 'This fucking piano's out of tune,' and made his exit. Paul Jones then came on to calm down the audience who were jeering loudly. The Who also threatened to cancel their appearance due to the faulty PA system but struggled on. (By the end of the tour, The Who were so desperate for amps that they were forced to borrow The Small Faces's equipment, which they then proceeded to destroy in their onstage act.)

There had been talk among the groups of cancelling this part of the tour in favour of a few days on the beach but the idea was scotched when it was pointed out that their audience would not tolerate a cancellation of any sort. Both Australia and New Zealand were, thanks to the British who had settled there, Mod strongholds. At all the Australian gigs, huge numbers of Mods had arrived on their scooters, dressed up to the nines. New Zealand promised more of the same. If the groups pulled out, full-scale rioting was a possibility, so the groups decided to continue the tour. They arrived in New Zealand in a boisterous and somewhat revengeful mood.

'We went beserk and took it out on them,' Marriott admitted. 'We wanted to get our own back. I remember once, all of us got in the swimming pool and just stayed in it all day in a great big bunch. No one else could get in. They were going to get us more bad publicity but it was only being stoned and having a laugh.

'It all started when EMI, who we went out there with, bought me a little portable record player for my birthday, my twenty-first, which was really sweet of them, and they gave me a bunch of records to play as well. Plus, I had the only suite in the hotel because it was my birthday. So they were really looking after me and making a fuss.

'There was me, Keith Moon, Pete Townshend, Ron and Wiggy [Peter Wolf], their roadie, who had his wig off, a brown egg top. We were all in the room for my birthday and I'd just opened my

Kenney Jones at the Logan Park Motor Hotel, Auckland, 30 January 1968.

present and put on this Stevie Wonder record. I still remember the track, "Baby Don't Do It", a Marvin Gaye thing that he did a great version of. Then, the record player started to feed back into itself. We were halfway through it and everyone's going for it and it goes wuurggh. So I bunged it out of the window – it was a mad moment – and off the balcony.

'So Wiggy ran down there, picked it up and brought it back up, all in bits, and he's thrown it over again. Well, it was the wrong thing to do in front of Keith Moon because the next thing that went out was the telly, armchairs, the lot went out of the window, the whole room.

'It wasn't sort of the hip thing to do back then. So it was just mad. It was dumb because the groups didn't do that then. I don't think anyone had done it, it was sort of a mad moment. Anyway, everything went out there and there was hysterical laughing, falling on the floor, until we realised what we'd done.

'There was an audience watching us down below, so we thought, what can we do? So I said, "I know, let's ring up and say someone's got in our room and, you know, destroyed our room and, to give it a bit of credibility, say they've nicked a couple of guitars."

'Because we thought, fucking hell, we can't own up to this. I mean the place was like, you know, everything was broke. So we rang down and up came the police and the management and all that, and we complained that our room had been broken into and smashed up.

'But Wiggy had been seen, you see, throwing these armchairs over the top, of course, with his bald head. You can't miss him. So he had to deny that he was the certain bald-headed man seen bunging settees over the balcony. The only bald-headed man in the hotel at the time.

'But we denied it, anyway, and incredibly we got away with it! Then EMI presented me with another

Wiggy (Who roadie), Pete Townshend and Steve in Auckland on Marriott's twenty-first birthday.

FAB 208 photo session. The pop process begins. Jimmy Winston is far left. Soon he will be out of the frame.

Ian McLagan's first photo session with the band. Ludgate Hill bombsite, November 1965.

SMALL FACES

'My Generation' style pose for the band.

Top: Bright lights, big city, fab gears. Bottom: 'Happy Boys Happy'.

The band with the look reflect on success.

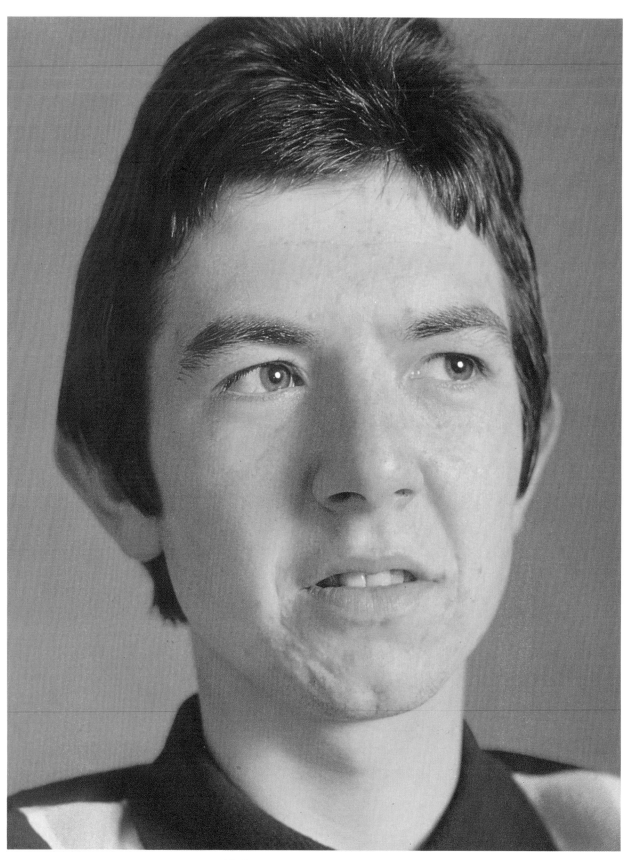

Early press shot of Ronnie Lane.

Kenney Jones circa 1966.

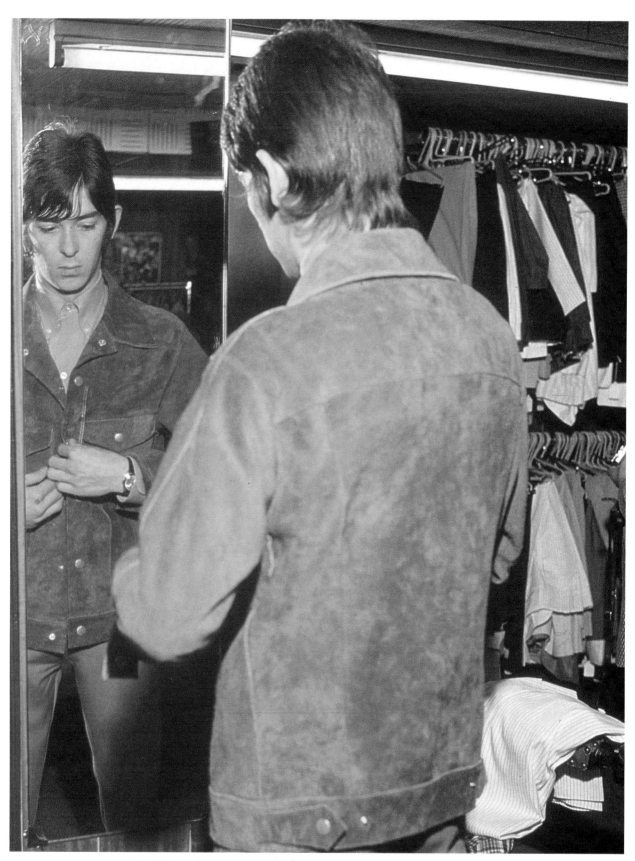

After joining the group, McLagan was quickly initiated into Modernism.

Steve Marriott and Ronnie Lane. One of the all-time great songwriting partnerships.

A fan sent the band four dummy crocodiles which made regular appearances in their photo sessions.

Shopping in Carnaby Street. The band were always mobbed on their frequent visits.

Putting on the style. Steve always looked great for the lens.

Ronnie Lane in action.

Fab 208 | The Small Faces

Great clothes, wrong bike.

Outside on the steps of the Rediffusion studios, circa 1966.

SMALL FACES

The East End's answer to The Beatles were often covered by *Rave*.

"MAC leaving? No — of course not!" groaned Stevie Marriott and Ronnie Lane in unison.

The mighty duo of the Small Faces were relaxing in their usual fashion at the offices of Immediate Records, sipping at welcome glasses of beer and jumping up and down to deafening stereophonic sounds.

But they were both surprised at the sudden wedding of their organist Ian 'Mac' McLagen to dancer Sandie Serjeant, last week, which had prompted the question.

Rumours had been circulating that all was not well within the Faces. But this was proved palpably untrue. Steve and Ronnie are still the best of working mates, and they have nothing but respect for Mac, and Kenny Jones, their drummer.

The Faces are working on a new British LP, have one due for America containing tracks like "Tin Soldier" and "Itchy Coo Park," and are going to Australia for a tour on January 12. They also hope to start a British tour in the spring.

"Yes, we're working hard, but it's a gas," said Steve. "There's nothing worse than sitting about on your backside getting bored."

Did Ronnie agree that groups' sound balance could do with some improvement?

"Our balance could be better. It's all according to what the hall is like. Open air places are terrible. Were you having a go at us? You've got to remember groups like Booker T and the MGs who everybody thought sounded just like the records, and older men, and much more professional than us.

"When things go wrong for us we just get the horrors. But half the promoters don't really cater for groups."

Was it true the Faces got a bad name for unreliability last year?

"Whenever we didn't turn up anywhere, I know for a fact we weren't supposed to be there anyway. You often get a promoter sending in a contract, which we haven't even seen, then find he has been advertising us for a week beforehand. They're trying to twist our arms, and we don't want it.

"Other times we haven't turned up either because we were ill or due to bad planning, like when we missed a plane to Paris. It's a terrible feeling when a lot of kids have been waiting for you, and we can't turn up. It's not a pleasant thing I know."

Stevie sipped his beer sadly and reflected on the thought that he has to move out of his new home at Chiswick, due to neighbour trouble.

"I've moved out into the country. I should have done it ages ago. The people who live on one side of me are great but the other side . . . she doesn't like me playing piano when I'm writing songs. She phoned up once and complained she couldn't hear Bach on the wireless.

"I want to get a cottage in the country like Stevie Winwood."

One more bit of trouble for Stevie, Ronnie, Kenny and Mac. As we chatted a telephone call came from BBC-TV to inform the group that the last line of their single " Tin Soldier " had to be cut out of a show, because it seemed to infer sleeping with a girl.

Stevie stiffened with anger for a bit then, slumped in his chair after hearing the news. "I actually said SIT with her, not sleep," he mumbled staring at his knees in perplexity.

"The meaning of the song is about getting into somebody's mind—not their body."

"It refers to a girl I used to talk to all the time, and she really gave me a buzz. The single was to give her a buzz in return and maybe other people as well. I dig it. There's no great message really, and no physical scenes."

The day the Faces can placate neighbours, producers and other grumblers, then they can really use the time honoured phrase "getting themselves together."—CHRIS WELCH

PLONK: 'It's a terrible feeling when a lot of kids have been waiting for you, and we can't turn up.'

First hint of discord in the camp, January 1968.

proper stereo after that, proper independent speakers, the lot. You've got to dig this though. They spend all day putting new french windows and doors on this suite and all new furniture gets put in it. This is all day.

'I'm out on the balcony with a bit of sun cream, keeping my head down and they're rebuilding the room. Builders are in and everything. So, come the evening, Keith came up again with Wolf and he said, "They've done a good job, haven't they?"

'DOSH! He's done it again. He's put another chair through the french windows and me and Wiggy looked at each other in amazement, and we scream, "No! No! No!" And he was going, "Yes! Yes! Yes!", bunging things out and smashing things. The whole room gets duffed up again. Fucking wrecked.

'Now we can't get away with it again and it also makes us right liars from the time before. So he rings

them down again – no, he didn't ring them up, they're banging on the door – that's right, it's the management. In they come and it's the manager in his dressing gown with his tie and shirt on.

'It was the highest building in Wellington, I think. It was one of the high-rise hotels. Anyway, he's come through the door steaming and he says, "Right, who done it?" Bastards and that sort of thing. We've all got a drink and Keith's got his tie and flicked it in his drink. He looks at him and said, "I fucking did it." Well, that didn't go down very well so they brought in the police to keep us in line, but we got them pissed.

'Instead of doing their job and keeping us under control they ended up going mad, drinking all the brandy. We were all wearing their big white helmets, dancing about. Well, they brought in the army after that. They got rid of the police and they had these geezers outside each one of our doors in short

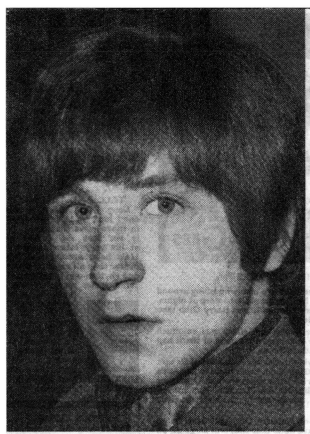

KENNY JONES

APRIL 1968						
SUN	MON	TUES	WED	THURS	FRI	SAT
*	1	2	3	4	5	6
7	8	9	10	11	12	13
14	15	16	17	18	19	20
21	22	23	24	25	26	27
28	29	30	*	*	*	*

MAY 1968						
SUN	MON	TUES	WED	THURS	FRI	SAT
*	*	*	1	2	3	4
5	6	7	8	9	10	11
12	13	14	15	16	17	18
19	20	21	22	23	24	25
26	27	28	29	30	31	*

JUNE 1968						
SUN	MON	TUES	WED	THURS	FRI	SAT
*	*	*	*	*	*	1
2	3	4	5	6	7	8
9	10	11	12	13	14	15
16	17	18	19	20	21	22

IT ALL HAPPENED TO KENNY

trousers with bolt loaders, like fucking big Lee Enfield muskets.

'You'd open the door and they'd go, "Get back in there," at gun point and that's a fact. So New Zealand was glad to see the back of us as well.'

Playing with The Who, however, brought home to the band the deficiencies in their live work. Townshend and Co. had been gigging constantly and their energy and attack outclassed and depressed the studio-bound Small Faces.

'I remember how good they were,' McLagan recalls, 'a really good band live, and we couldn't match it. We were playing "Itchycoo Park" at the time and at the hotel we had taped the sound of the jets flying above. We took the cassette, I miked it up and when we went into the song, I would press play and that was how we got the effect for it live. Technology was great in those days.'

To add insult to injury, at the concert in Wellington, Townshend borrowed a pink Fender Stratocaster that had been presented to Marriott by all the bands to mark his twenty-first birthday. Townshend then demolished the guitar on stage.

Still, at least some good came out of the disaster-prone tour – the chorus line for their next single was written during their stay. Chris Neill, who hung out with the groups, reports that, 'The woo-de-doo-de-doo chorus in "Lazy Sunday" was a drunken chant that the groups would sing to each other. "R-e-e-b" (beer spelt backwards) was another favourite.'

The last comment goes to *The Truth*, a New Zealand newspaper. 'We don't want them back again,' it thundered. 'They are just unwashed, foul-smelling, booze-swilling no-hopers.'

On their return to Britain the band hired out some boats and took to the Thames waterway. The idea was to create some time and space for Marriott and Lane to finish writing their third album. Work on it had begun in 1967 and songs, such as 'Rollin' Over', had already been incorporated into the live set. As much of the music had been written and recorded, the four days on the boats were to be given over to lyric writing. No thematic link between the new material had as yet been established. Until one night, in a less than sober mood, either Marriott or Lane had looked up at the half-moon beaming

down on them and rhetorically asked where the other part of it was. The germ of an idea was thus planted.

'The story,' Ronnie Lane told John Pidgeon in a Radio One interview, 'is a kind of mystical journey. There's this kid, who kind of falls in love with the moon, and all of a sudden he observes the moon being eaten away by time. You know the way they go, they wax and wane, don't they? And of course when it's gone, he's all down; and then the thing is that all of a sudden – boosh! – it comes back again, like life itself. And I thought that was something to pick up on really, because you can often get brought down by something, and you're just being stupidly impatient usually.'

A year previously *Sgt Pepper* had been hailed as the first ever concept album although this in itself was misleading. Paul McCartney may have wanted to make the album the story of an alter ego band but only a handful of the tracks relate to the main Sgt Pepper character. Despite this, the 'concept' album, in which all the songs portray a story and

Marriott with his first wife, Jenny Rylands.

Gered Mankowitz shot taken at Steve's Chiswick flat, 1968.

characters, was the latest artistic craze, a genre that Pete Townshend would later bring to full fruition with The Who's *Tommy* album.

Marriott and Lane were intrigued by the idea but they had reservations. They believed that a whole album dedicated to one theme would not sustain itself, stretching the listener's patience too far. Instead, they opted to make one side of their album the story of Happiness Stan (Lane's father's name) and his search for the other half of the moon, while the first side would contain all new but unrelated songs.

117

Steve Marriott's Diary

SUNDAY

GOT UP today because it was a nice day and the sun was shining. Sat and looked out the window for an hour. Decided to take the dogs for a walk. I've got three dogs and six cats. Well, to tell the truth, I arrived at this house with one cat—but you know what cats are!

The dogs are a groove. There's an Alsatian called Lucy, a Collie called Shamus and a Whippet called Love. They like watching football on the telly. Groovy dogs. Trouble is if I don't take them out they get very athletic and leap around on me bed—which isn't a groove.

Came back, fed the dogs, then fed me on jacket potatoes and salad. Went round to Ronnie's to rehearse because we're doing Greenford Starlight Ballroom tonight and it's the first time we're doing "Lazy

Sunday" onstage. We used acoustic guitar on the record, but for the stage we use electric, and unless you're careful you get a lot of feedback problems. Very technical. Also very annoying.

Doesn't worry me that it's Easter Sunday and everyone else's on holiday while we're working. I'd rather be on holiday when everyone else is working — otherwise you go for a walk and the park's full of draggy people.

Back home again! We played well. We like playing there 'cos the ceiling's low and the stage is low and we get a good sound going. Me old mate Keith Moon came to watch us and afterwards said "Right off to the Speakeasy for a quick one." Yes, we thought, good idea. We always have problems getting out the dressing room there and tonight was no exception. A bird got hold of me barnet (hair, to the uninitiated) and nearly ripped it all out. She had a grip like iron, couldn't get her off, and then another one got hold of Kenny. It's a shame really 'cos birds like that can spoil the whole evening for you. I was shattered and had a thumping great headache by the time we got away.

Got to the Speakeasy, rushed for the bar and then—disaster!

Remembered it was Sunday and licensing laws won't allow booze after 11 p.m., so we got real bored and had pineapple juice and took the mickey out of a few people and left.

TUESDAY

MONDAY disappeared in a haze—so on to Tuesday. Quite a normal day for me. Got up at 11 a.m. and went shopping in Chiswick. I like shopping there 'cos people won't believe it. " Chiswick ? " they say, "What sort of a place is that to go shopping?" It's groovy really. I bought some groceries 'cos the vegetable man called before I left and I bought some stuff off him. Oh! and I bought a gas little Indian cane table.

Went home and got a bit smashed and then Ronnie said: "Come round" so I did, and Pete Townshend was there, which was a loon 'cos I haven't seen him for years. Had a natter about America and our disaster trip to Australia—which was the last time we met.

WEDNESDAY

GOT UP at 1 p.m.—getting over hangover of night before. Had a bath and washed me barnet. Oh yes, I'm very clean. Denny, our road manager who used to be with The Truth and is a real groove, came and picked me up to go round to Ronnies. Then on to a photo session for some stuff for Decca. Finished that and decided we NEEDED a drink—takes it out of you, photo sessions.

Full of good intentions decided to start out early for our date in Stevenage. Unfortunately got side-tracked and three hours later arrived at date. Well, we were an hour early but Dennis hadn't got the equipment set up and I broke me guitar, so by the time he repaired that and got us organised it was time to start anyway.

Didn't play well. Forgot to tell you but at Greenford some nasty wily so-and-so nicked Ronnie's good amplifier and substituted for it a lousy one. So Ronnie had a hard time on stage coping with whistling and screeching from the amp, and when that happens we go to pieces. We're not a group that can cope with drama like that —if we know the sound's wrong it makes us bad tempered.

THURSDAY

Ronnie: writing

GOT UP ear 'cos I had to some interviev then we wei to recordi studios to c tracks for LP. We're usi a new pla called Tride 'cos it's ve hard to fi good recordi studios in Lo don. We used to love Olymp but it's always so booked u it's ridiculous.

Ronnie and I have writte 20 new numbers for the albu and we're going to cut P Arnold's "If You Think You'! Groovy," in a new way. Tl reason Ronnie and I manage to get so many songs togeth is that we went away for th weekend a little while ago.

We're going again this wee! end for four days. It's a re gas—unbelievable! We hire th eight-berth boat and go up rive and directly we crunch our wa into a nice quiet lock we pla Mothers Of Invention albun full blast and ruin the pea of the countryside. We're ve; destructive really, but at lea we come off with some stu written, which is better tha nothing!

Marriott's diary. Monday, apparently, 'disappeared in a haze'.

'Every band at that point,' Glyn Johns explains, 'were all trying to keep up with or go one better than everybody else with new sounds. It was an exploratory period, breaking out from the use of very standard instruments and recording techniques. They were all trying to stretch the limits and that was started by The Beatles with *Sgt Pepper* and the use of LSD.

'The Small Faces were very much into LSD and they made it work. Not from my point of view because I've never taken an aspirin, I'm one of the world's bores . . . Interestingly enough, I never really noticed a lot of the time who was on what, I just got on with it. It got a bit boring sometimes because people would drift off and become unintelligible but the fact of the matter was that everyone I worked with during that period pushed me to come up with new sounds and ideas that I probably wouldn't have done without them. I got the benefit of their drug-taking without the risks to the brain.'

With the storyline established, the band's third album got underway with the group insisting on recording in numerous studios to find the best

sound possible. It would take them many months to complete the work, but it would definitely be worth the wait.

To precede it, a single, 'Lazy Sunday'/'Rollin' Over', was released on 5 April. It shot straight into the charts at number two.

'We don't really want a number one because it puts so many obligations upon you. People expect too much. Anyway, we've been banned from so many places because we're too loud. That's why we aren't doing a tour. We'd like to but we got banned after the Roy Orbison tour. But despite everything, including the bad reputation, we are surviving. There's nothing we can do about a reputation because it's something given to us by other people.'

STEVE MARRIOTT, APRIL 1968

'We didn't want to release "Lazy Sunday" as a single,' Marriott confessed, 'even though we virtually knew it would be a hit. We didn't want those gimmicky things to be a trademark; we'd just done "Itchycoo Park". The effects made us laugh but we

New Musical Express

EVERY FRIDAY 7D

HOLLIES, CLIFF AND FANS

Monkees new LP Track by track

Andy Williams
Show Stoppers
Paper Dolls

DAVE DEE CARTOON

TOP POP NEWS

JOHN ROWLES PIC SPECIAL

No. 1111   Week ending April 27, 1968
WORLD'S **LARGEST** CIRCULATION OF **ANY** MUSIC PAPER

LAZY SUNDAY. SMALL FACES

IMMEDIATE IM004

Kennedy Street Enterprises Ltd., and Peter Walsh present

International Hit Recorders

HERMANS HERMITS

"Bend Me, Shake Me"
MEN CORNER

PAPER DOLLS
"Something Here in My Heart"

DAVE BERRY

THE ECHOES

JOHN ROWLES
Guest Star—"If I only had time"

T.V. Favourite...
JOHNNY BALL

BIRMINGHAM. TOWN HALL	FRIDAY, MAY 10th, 6.30 & 8.45	LEEDS. ODEON	WEDNESDAY, MAY 15th, 6.0 & 8.30
IPSWICH. GAUMONT	SATURDAY, MAY 11th, 6.35 & 8.45	LINCOLN. A.B.C.	THURSDAY, MAY 16th, 6.15 & 8.30
SLOUGH. ADELPHI	SUNDAY, MAY 12th, 6.0 & 8.30	WIGAN. A.B.C.	FRIDAY, MAY 17th, 6.20 & 8.35
MAIDSTONE. GRANADA	MONDAY, MAY 13th, 6.20 & 8.30	BLACKPOOL. A.B.C.	SATURDAY, MAY 18th, 6.10 & 8.45
WORCESTER. GAUMONT	TUESDAY, MAY 14th, 6.15 & 8.45	NOTTINGHAM. THEATRE ROYAL	SUNDAY, MAY 19th, 5.30 & 8.0

119

Rare studio shot of the band recording 'Lazy Sunday'.

'Do we feel "Lazy Sunday" points a way to The Small Faces's direction? Well, to be honest, I don't believe in direction as a word. The most you can do is try to make each record progressively better than the last. I think groups who say, "I think we've progressed," are talking a lot of rubbish. Other people should be able to listen to your music and tell you whether you've got better – it's not for you to say. Anyway, if you concentrate on just progressing then there's something wrong with your group.'

STEVE MARRIOTT, APRIL 1968

took ourselves kind of seriously, though you'd never know it from those singles. On "Itchycoo Park" we had about six engineers with four machines all running together so we could just phase the drums rather than the whole thing.

'We had some damn good ideas. We used to rub the engineers up the wrong way. They'd think we were little smart-arses saying, "Look, we want this,"

and if we didn't get it right, we'd say, "No, that's not what we want.

'Originally there were so many sounds we wanted to get going but just couldn't. You have to leave it all to the engineer to begin with and tell him what you want. It takes such a long time to learn. It's just a case of going to more and more recording sessions and hanging around the studio learning.'

STEVE MARRIOTT ON PRODUCING
'ITCHYCOO PARK', AUTUMN 1967

'They'd say, "You can't do that, it's untechnical, unethical and it's not in the manual" – such as putting tracks out of synch for various effects. Everybody uses those effects today.'

It was not only the music for 'Lazy Sunday' that triggered such a massive response. Undoubtedly, its classic British subject matter – of interfering neighbours – captured people's imaginations.

'"Lazy Sunday" was about Steve's neighbours in

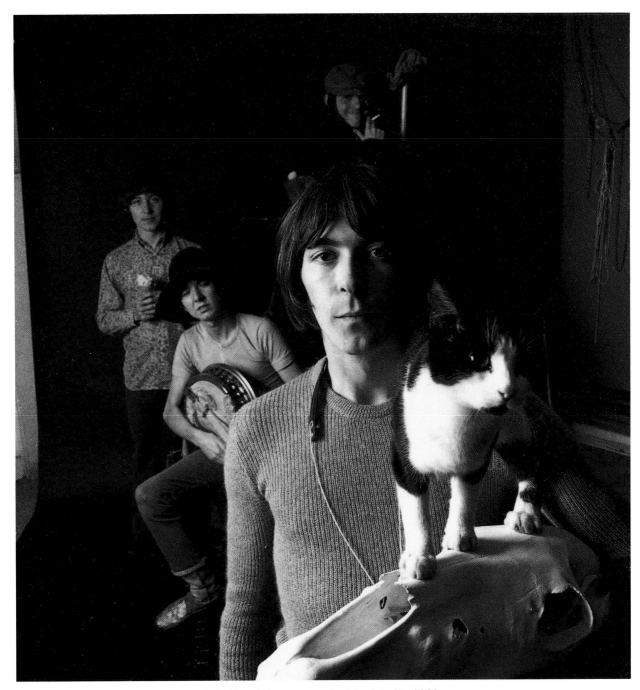

The Small Faces pose for Mankowitz, 1968.

Chiswick, well, *all* his neighbours really,' Kenney Jones explains. 'Wherever he went they all complained about him and he was forever having to move. But this was about the one in Chiswick. He had moved into this huge house by the Thames, a beautiful Victorian terrace house, and they were forever banging on the walls complaining about the noise and his dog that shat everywhere.

'Until one day our roadie spiked the water tank that supplied the whole row with acid. You couldn't even clean your teeth for weeks afterwards.'

Marriott, who had brought in a friend to decorate one wall of his Chiswick sitting room with a massive painting of the cartoon character Thor, supposedly wrote the lyrics on the toilet one day. He and Lane then produced the song.

121

Steve's Chiswick pad. A friend painted Thor on the wall.

'I wrote the tune ["Lazy Sunday"] in the khazi – it's true! Pretty strange, I know.'

STEVE MARRIOTT, APRIL 1968

'Everyone thought Andrew Oldham was producing us,' Marriott recalled. 'I remember a conversation with Graham Nash when he was with The Hollies, waiting to go on *Top Of The Pops*. He said, "I like what Andrew's doing on 'Lazy Sunday'." I said, "What the fuck are you talking about? That's us!" After that, I got lots of offers to produce other people, me and Ronnie separately. We took up a couple but very rarely. One thing I liked, which I never got credit for, was "Supernatural Fairy Tale", the title track of the album by Art [who became Spooky Tooth]. They wanted the phasing and that shit, so I did it. It came out as "Produced by Jimmy Miller", who'd done the rest of the LP.'

'When Steve played us "Lazy Sunday" it was a ballad,' McLagan remembers, "and I hated it. It was only when he started doing all these stupid things in the studio on it that it got any good.'

'When we first cut the record ["Lazy Sunday"] every-one thought it was a laugh. Steve started singing it in the recording studio and began to laugh at the song. Then we all began laughing at it. It was really quite a straight song to begin with until Steve started chucking in "Inky Pinky Poos" for a giggle. When we finished it we all thought it was very funny. But we had no intention of releasing it.'

IAN McLAGAN, MAY 1968

To augment the album's storyline, Marriott and Lane had decided to bring in the eccentric English actor, Stanley Unwin, to narrate the Happiness Stan story. Their first choice had been the comedian Spike Milligan but, surprisingly, he had turned them down.

Unwin's speciality was his stylish corruption of the English language into his own inventive slang, an art that Marriott and Lane felt was perfect for their 'concept'. Subsequently, the actor spent time with the group in various studios, quietly picking up on their verbal codes and sayings which he later incorporated into his final story.

'It made us laugh,' Marriott said. 'Anything that made us laugh we liked. God knows how it worked but it did and I'm very proud of it, and the other Small Faces are too. It was worth the year's work. We recorded backing tracks over and over in different studios to see which was the best and rewrote the words and got crazy Stanley Unwin in to narrate it. We gave him a glossary of hip terms to throw in with the Cockneyisms. The editing alone took three months. It's timeless to me. A lot of people remember it too, which also obviously makes it worthwhile. I still play it if I can find a good copy.'

'I can remember sessions at Trident and I can remember sessions at IBC,' Glyn Johns recalls. 'I know we did Stanley Unwin's bit at Olympic Studios. I don't remember it taking a long time. It might have been done over a long period of time because it was a concept album and they had to figure out how to put it all together. By that I mean physically how to tie it together, the use of sound effects and all the rest of it. That would have been a culmination of all their ideas and my ideas but the concept was obviously theirs, nothing to do with me at all.'

'Really this album [Ogdens'] is just the beginning of things. We're now free to do exactly what we want and Ronnie and Steve are into different things. We are not going to make the mistake of getting in one bag and getting stuck there – that's what happened to groups like The Searchers.'

KENNEY JONES, JULY 1968

'Ogdens' Nut Gone Flake', the album's title track and opening song, was actually an instrumental version of their old Decca single, 'I Got Mine', using only piano, bass and drums, and a wah-wah pedal attached to Ian McLagan's keyboard (whenever he struck a chord, Marriott, who was standing in the control room, operated the effect).

The next track, the tremendous 'Afterglow', was ruined for Marriott by his lyrics ('Lovely track, shame about the words') while 'Long Agos and Worlds Apart' was McLagan's contribution. He remembers it as 'a waffling song', a mix of swirling effects that acts as a bridge between the red-hot soul of 'Afterglow' and the pub sing-along knees-up of Marriott and Lane's musically hilarious 'Rene'.

This song was about Rene Tungate, a woman Marriott had known when he was growing up in Strone Road, Manor Park. (She actually did give birth to children of every size and colour.) The song is laced with typical Small Faces humour and evokes an East End Saturday night party with everyone gathered around the piano, raucously singing the praises of this colourful local character. For Lane, laughter made the world go round, a philosophy equally shared by the rest of the group. But Lane's other philosophy mystified them.

123

With the advent of LSD, many users had been exposed to spiritual experiences. In 1967, singer Billy Nicholls had converted Lane to the teachings of the Indian guru, Meher Baba, and, on their ill-fated Australian tour, he in turn had influenced Pete Townshend to follow the same route to enlightenment. Consequently, Lane's composition 'Song Of A Baker', the album's next track, was inspired by a Sufi book he had been reading. Musically, it was early heavy metal, a far cry from the peace and tranquillity required for contemplation. It is not documented whether Lane had already heard Marriott's composition 'Wham Bam Thank You Mam', which

'The secret of nearly all our records now is that we are really just being ourselves – that's what it's all about.'

STEVE MARRIOTT, AUGUST 1968

Hats and horses. Kenney with the boys, circa 1968.

would surface later that year, but the two songs not only bear a striking similarity but preview Marriott's later direction with Humble Pie. Both can hardly be considered classic material.

As the crashing chords of 'Baker' fade into the distance the distinctive keyboard coda of 'Lazy Sunday' enters and the hit single finishes off the first side.

The 'concept' side opens up with Stanley Unwin's narrative, which is interspersed between each track, leading into Marriott's 'Happiness Stan', which was written on the keyboard using some 'very moody little chords'.

Unwin reappears before the band charge into 'Rollin' Over', a thunderous R & B mixture of guitar and organ, topped off by Marriott's powerful vocals. For some time the song had actually been called 'Bun In The Oven'. The brass section was supplied by Eddie Thornton, who was working with Georgie Fame at the time, and who later went on to do a mini tour with The Small Faces.

For Lane's next song, 'The Hungry Intruder', the band brought in four musicians from a top London orchestra. They were conducted by actor David McCallum's father, John. To write the strings arrangement, Marriott and Lane would figure out the melody on a mellotron and have the music transcribed on to paper which would then be given to the musicians.

As the end of the story approached, the band had to figure out a satisfactory conclusion. Happiness Stan has by now met a fly who is accompanying him on his quest. 'The Journey' represented the fly's departure before Stan meets up with 'Mad John', the song's title inspired by one of Don Arden's employees. Marriott, who wrote the tune, no doubt remembered the day he was introduced to 'Mad Tom' in Arden's office. Marriott had greeted him using first names only. The burly minder had picked Marriott up by his collar and told him, in no uncertain terms, 'Mad Tom to you!'

The album's closing song, 'Happy Days Toy Town', was a rare all-group composition. At a loss as to how to resolve all the story's strands, they decided, in true East End tradition, that Happiness Stan should meet the man who tells him about the

moon, at which point a knees-up ensues, with Unwin exhorting all the listeners to 'stay cool, man'.

The album was released on 24 May. It went straight in at number one and stayed there for six weeks. Public and critics alike raved about it.

To promote it, Immediate issued an advert which parodied The Lord's Prayer, extolling the group's musical virtues. It caused a predictable uproar in the press, as outraged readers wrote in to complain, and the band were quick to absolve themselves of any responsibility.

'We didn't know a thing about the ad until we saw it in the music papers. And frankly we got the horrors at first. We realise that it could be taken as a serious knock against religion. But on thinking it over, we don't feel it is particularly good or bad. It's just another form of advertising. We're not all that concerned about it. We're more concerned in writing our music and producing our records.'

STEVE MARRIOTT ON THE ADVERT FOR *OGDENS' NUT GONE FLAKE* THAT PARODIED THE LORD'S PRAYER, JUNE 1968

The other outstanding feature of the album was its sleeve. Apparently inspired by Ronnie Lane, the LP was imaginatively packaged in an elaborate round fold-out sleeve, which resembled a tobacco tin. It was a gimmick but also an in-joke. Smokers of the herb often kept their 'stash' in tobacco tins, and the words 'Nut Gone' in the title, along with a picture of king-size rolling papers with the word 'Sus' written on them, need no further explanation. The cover deservedly received several design awards.

'The album is re-issued every couple of years somewhere,' Marriott stated. 'They've even gotten to where they've put a picture of the original round cover on the front of a square cover – after all we went through to get it right. [The original jacket was five connected circles, twelve and a quarter inches in diameter which folded up to resemble a tin of Ogdens' Nut Gone Flake Tobacco.] We cleaned up every award in the book for it and Andrew collected them. We caught him on the stairs of Immediate's office, his arms full of bits of plastic – "Best

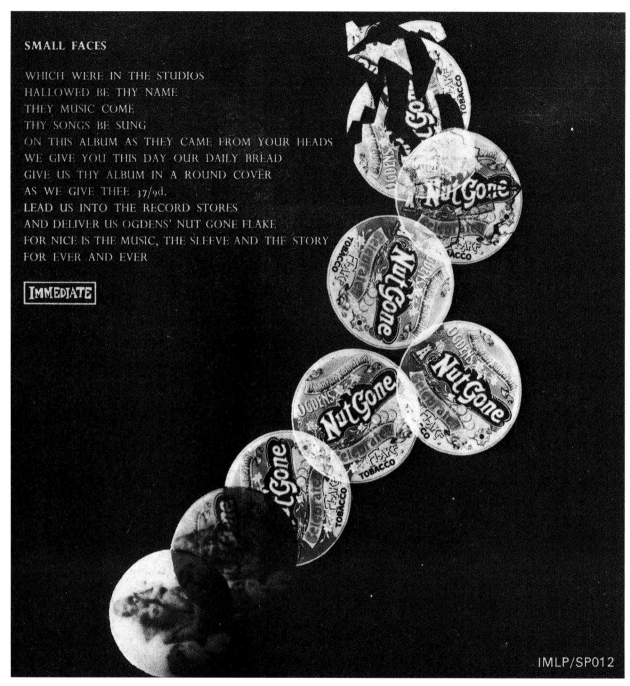

SMALL FACES

WHICH WERE IN THE STUDIOS
HALLOWED BE THY NAME
THEY MUSIC COME
THY SONGS BE SUNG
ON THIS ALBUM AS THEY CAME FROM YOUR HEADS
WE GIVE YOU THIS DAY OUR DAILY BREAD
GIVE US THY ALBUM IN A ROUND COVER
AS WE GIVE THEE 37/9d.
LEAD US INTO THE RECORD STORES
AND DELIVER US OGDENS' NUT GONE FLAKE
FOR NICE IS THE MUSIC, THE SLEEVE AND THE STORY
FOR EVER AND EVER

IMMEDIATE

IMLP/SP012

The controversial advert for *Ogdens' Nut Gone Flake*, June 1968.

Artwork", "Best Design", "Best Album". We said, "Where the fuck did you get all those?" His face went crimson. Bless his heart; I suppose someone had to get them – he knew we wouldn't – but we just gave him a little grief anyway.'

With the material displaying both their awesome power, on tracks such as 'Rollin' Over' and 'Afterglow', and their mixing of psychedelia with Cockney singalongs, to hilarious effect, on 'Rene' or 'Mad John', the band easily achieved their twin targets of critical acceptance and commercial success.

Yet complex doubts still lingered in Marriott's mind. He hated the group's pop tag. What's more, the success of *Ogdens'* seemed to frighten him – at some point he would have to come up with a follow-up that was of a higher standard. He was also,

1968: own up time

Small Faces advert starts furore

by Laurie Henshaw

IN their never-ending quest for eye-catching gimmicks, you never know what those Ad Boys will get up to next.

Now, a storm is buzzing around the unsuspecting heads of the Small Faces. All over that parody of the Lord's Prayer in the MM on June 1.

For it went thisaway: "Small Faces — which were in the studio, hallowed by thy name, thy music come, thy songs be sung." And so on.

ADVERTISING

All in the cause of advertising the latest Small Faces album, "Ogden's Nut Gone Celebrated Flake."

And what a who-ha it triggered off. Admitted a spokesman for Immediate Records: "There has been a lot of comment about it. But we didn't write it. We borrowed it from God. We merely changed the words a bit."

One gentleman who objected to the advert in the MM was P. R. Dawes, of Kings College, Taunton, Somerset.

Dipping his pen in vitriol, he blasted: "How dare these exponents of popular codswallop presume upon something dear, and very real, to countless millions of people?

"I refer to the disgusting, deplorable, nauseating, sickening, base, vulgar and pretentious way in which the Small Faces have dared to interpret the Lord's Prayer in advertising their latest mass wax wastage.

CONCERNED

"This must surely rank with the sacrilegious crime of the decade for these four 'musicians' to associate themselves and their 'music' with anything as beautiful and perfect as the Lord's Prayer."

Strong words, indeed. But words that call for a reply from Small Face Steve Marriott.

Says Steve: "We didn't know a thing about the ad until we saw it in the music papers. And frankly, we got the horrors at first. We realise it could be taken as a serious knock against religion.

"But on thinking it over, we don't feel it is either particularly good or bad. It's just another form of advertising. We don't particularly agree or disagree with it. We're not all that concerned about it. We're more concerned in writing our music and producing our records. We have nothing to do with the publicity.

RELIGIOUS

"But I must admit I thought the advert a bit cheeky. I only hope it doesn't go any further.

"I think most people will consider it as just an advert, and nothing more.

"That chap who wrote to the MM obviously goes to church and is a very religious man. I'm sorry he was so upset. And he obviously doesn't like groups.

"Personally, I'm not that much concerned about religion. I haven't been to church since I was a choirboy. I realised then religion wasn't for me. We attended weddings and funerals, and it was all such a bore.

"But if people want to be religious, that's their business. There will always be people who have to have something to believe in.

"Me? I just believe in life. Life goes on."

Small Faces labeled disgusting, distasteful and other goodies...

THEY should be banned from ever making another record! He should be banned from being a publicist! They should be taken to court and their names scandalised the world over and they should be excommunicated from whichever religious denomination they belong to (if any)! Who am I talking about? — The SMALL FACES and their PUBLICIST! It must surely be an accepted fact, by now, that pop singers, much as they may dislike it, ARE moral leaders to their hero-worshipping, ignorant fans. What kind of moral leadership is the advert promoting the latest Faces album? This is the advert: "Small Faces, Which were in their studios, Hallowed be thy name, Thy music come, Thy song be sung, On this album as they come from your heads, We give you this our daily bread, Give us thy album in a round cover, As we give thee 37/9. Lead us into thy record stores and deliver us 'Ogden's Nut Gone Flake', For nice is the music the sleeve and the story, For ever and ever." Just how disgusting and distasteful can you get? What are they trying to do — cripple the new generation's acceptance of Christianity? — a subject about which they themselves apparently know nothing. If they did they would never display such ignorance as this mockery of the Lord's prayer. I hope the authorities seize on this as their opportunity to put a censorship on sensation seeking publicity and that the people concerned offer a public apology. Nigel P. Heatley, 1 Brixton Terrace, Penrose Road, Helston, Cornwall.

Val: 'Disgusting and distasteful' or just good humour to the majority?

at this juncture, concerned about the group's humour which was becoming something of a double-edged sword.

Though desperate to be taken seriously, the band could never resist inserting jokes, be they musical or otherwise, into their work. It was a compulsion that brought them many admirers but at the same time partly served to mask their genuine musical talent and versatility. While people smiled, Marriott reasoned, the true art passed them by. It was an artistic cul-de-sac of their own making.

Even so, Kenney Jones was eager to capitalise on the album by taking it out on the road. His idea was to make it a live extravaganza with Stanley Unwin narrating and the band employing a brass section to flesh out the songs. But the tour never happened. The complexities of the music coupled with the effects needed to bring it to life seemed beyond the grasp of the group. After all, live performances were not their forte and Marriott, especially, was aware of this chink in their armour.

Instead Marriott appeared on an Easybeats track, 'Good Times' (from their *Virgil* album), before the group went in to help write and record the aforementioned album for Immediate singer, Billy Nicholls.

Marriott's next move was to present the band with a new song that he had just written in his back garden. Although no one knew it at the time, 'The Universal'/'Donkey Rides, A Penny A Glass' would prove to be the band's last official single.

'It ["The Universal"] would have made a beautiful LP track but as a single it was destined to be a "limbo record" just touching the top twenty. If my mother can't understand a record then I know it's not commercial.'

STEVE MARRIOTT, OCTOBER 1968

It reached sixteen in the charts, a disappointing placing after 'Lazy Sunday', but a crushing blow to its creator who believed it was the best song he had ever written, especially the lyrics which dwelled upon, in an oblique way, his feelings about stardom (Mick Jagger is mentioned towards the song's end). Compared with the bright and full sound the group

127

YOUR MONTHLY ALBUM GUIDE

OGDENS Nut Gone Celebrated FLAKE

Faces—gimmick is justified by the music

IN case you hadn't noticed, the Small Faces are no longer a teenybopper group relying on the effervescent charm of Steve Marriott to keep the girlish screams at full volume.

SMALL FACES: " Ogden's Nut Gone Flake." Ogden's Nut Gone Flake; Afterglow; Long Agos And Worlds Apart; Rene; Song Of A Baker; Lazy Sunday); Happiness Stan (Happiness Stan; Rollin' Over; The Hungry Intruder; The Journey; Mad John; Happydaystoytown).

DEVELOPED

They have, in fact, developed into one of the most rewarding groups on the British scene, continually trying new things yet retaining contact with the public. Between them, they have also developed into a real force as songwriters.

This album got plenty of publicity on the strength of it's novel, round sleeve with it's reproduction of a Victorian tobacco tin. But, for once, the gimmick is justified by the music.

VERSATILITY

The Faces have come up with two suites — one on each side of the album. Each is divided into six tracks which cover a remarkably wide range of sounds and show the group's unusual versatility — both as performers and writers. There is a constant flow of ideas and some of the lyrics have just the right blend of originality and humour — how about " Life is just a bowl of All Bran"?

" Ogden's " the first suite, includes their successful single " Lazy Sunday " and another of Steve's cockney bits " Rene " all about the daughter of a docker.

" Happiness Stan " the best of the two, ends with a brilliant send-up track, " Happydaystoytown." Each theme or this suite is introduced by Stanley Unwin whose double talk is effective enough first time through, but tends to pall a bit with repeated playing.

EXCELLENT

The whole album is pop of a very high order and the arrangements are first class, full of varied sounds. There is good use of a string section and some excellent guitar work as well as neat organ on " Stan."

A thoroughly deserving LP Of The Month. — BOB DAWBARN.

POP LP OF THE MONTH

Headline says it all – Faces – gimmick music. A popular perception.

had achieved on their landmark singles, 'The Universal' sounds like an anti-single, a perverse blow against their audience's expectations. The music is partly muddied and the attitude in the playing almost throwaway.

'People keep saying that "Universal" is a send-up of Dylan or the one-man-band – they don't seem to realise that it's a serious record. Which proves that they don't really listen to it because if they did they'd understand what it's all about. It's about getting up in the morning and going outside and saying hello to the Universe.'

STEVE MARRIOTT, AUGUST 1968

'It was recorded on a cassette in my back garden,' Marriott explained. 'That's why you hear dogs barking and everything. One of the funniest things I have ever written. People loved it because it was very tongue-in-cheek, very English word-association thing.'

'We didn't know it was going to be the last single,' Jones notes. 'Steve had recorded the vocal on a little tape recorder sitting in his garden playing guitar. You can hear the traffic going by and his dogs almost barking on cue – musical dogs! We

finished it off in the studio and we all played on it using the same vocal.

'I recorded it there in the garden with the dogs about me and you can even hear Jenny shouting, "Hello, Steve," as she came back through the gate from shopping.'

STEVE MARRIOTT, AUGUST 1968

'Steve was incredibly fed up at that point. He hated us still being labelled as a pop band, especially after the success of *Ogdens'*. It was almost as if he didn't want to follow it up, like he was frightened we couldn't top it, and I think it shows he'd ·had a taste of other things by then and he wanted to go off and play with the big boys, if you like. But we didn't know that at the time of "The Universal". With hindsight, we should have seen something was definitely on the cards.'

Marriott's lifestyle had changed during this

'You know, we'd really like to do some of those free concerts in Hyde Park that The Traffic have been doing recently but we'd get all "toughies" from Finchley who would come along to start a fight.'

STEVE MARRIOTT, AUGUST 1968

WE DID 'UNIVERSAL' IN 30 MINUTES!

STEVE MARRIOTT TALKS TO RMs DEREK BOLTWOOD

STEVE MARRIOTT

"The Universal" says Steve is really a serious song. All those who accused him of sending up Dylan or trying to copy the Byrds, repent!

TIME for breakfast at the Marriott household with the sun shining down and the Faces and a dozen house guests and half a dozen assorted dogs all grooving in the garden and eating bacon and eggs.

Thus, in an ancient mansion in the deepthest deeps of Buckinghamshire the Small Faces' "Universal" was born. Within half an hour of sitting out in the five acre garden, the song had been written and recorded.

"We had the idea for the song," explained Steve, "but we wrote it and recorded the vocal within the space of about thirty minutes. The vocal track on the record is actually the one we recorded in the garden that morning — we tried it again in the studio when it came to making the disc, but it just didn't sound right. It wasn't as spontaneous — and of course we didn't have the dogs barking, and they're really an important part of the record. My voice is far more natural on that first recording than on any of the studio tracks as well.

"People keep saying that 'Universal' is a send up of Dylan, or the one man band, or anything in fact — they don't seem to realise that it's a serious record. Which proves that they don't really listen to it, because if they did they'd understand what it's all about. It's about getting up in the morning and going outside and saying hello to the Universe. And it greets you—like the line 'Goodmorning Steve, you won't believe me today'. It's very simple really—but it's far from being a send-up. 'Lazy Sunday' was, and I suppose a lot of people think this one must be because of our last

record — but it's nothing like it in fact. It was incredible when we recorded it because there were so many people there, and all these dogs rushing around and barking. Anyway we got a finished tape out of it, and all we had to do was add backings and things.

"I think it's best to get things done quickly, and spontaneously, like that. Groups who say that it's taken them nine months to record a number are really wasting their time — I'm sure if they tried they could get it done in half the time — and probably get a better result as well. You can work on a number for ages — you know, writing and getting ideas and things. But when you're actually recording it, I think it's good to work to a deadline. Like our album, "Nut Gone" — we had the idea for that for a year, but when it came to putting the tracks down we set ourselves a deadline and kept to it. Every day we'd work on it, and things would get better — but it wasn't until the very last day that everything fell into place, like a jigsaw puzzle. Previously we couldn't quite get it together, but on the last day we recorded it in one go, and it worked. But I'm sure that if we didn't have a deadline, we'd have gone on recording and never really have got anywhere.

HOUSE IN THE COUNTRY

"Ronnie and I have moved out into this great house out in Buckinghamshire — right in the country, with a five acre garden and a wood in the grounds. I could never live in London again — the atmosphere is so different. We do a lot of work there, but it doesn't seem like work — there's nothing else to do. There are no distractions or anything — I just find myself writing very naturally without having to force myself to work. We hope to be getting a new place in the country in the near future, and then perhaps we can start to record there. Perhaps build a studio or something.

"We've been making this film for Top of the Pops at the place in Buckinghamshire. It's just us and the dogs and everybody just doing things in the garden of this house — and the guy who's made the film shot a lot of pictures of everything. There wasn't a real story — but by cutting the film afterwards and putting different sequences together, we can put a story to it. At the moment there are about five different story-lines that we can use by putting together different parts of the film.

RECORDED IN GARDEN

"It's a great way of doing it — it's not professional filming perhaps. Well, not in the way it was made — there are no clapper boys running around shouting "Scene one, Take seventy" or anything like that. But what does it matter if we didn't film it in the traditional, professional manner? As long as the result is good. It's like it doesn't matter that we recorded part of our new single on a tape recorder in the garden, because the result is good. I don't like the idea of doing things in the straight professional way that's always been accepted just because that's the "right" way. It's too restrictive — you're always bound by show-business traditions.

"There are a lot of people all over the world who are doing great things in filming, recording, acting and so on — and they're doing things in their own way, not in the "show-business tradition". And what's good is that they're now being accepted. The barriers are gradually being broken down, and a lot of groovy people with groovy ideas are making a name for themselves. When all these people start working together and swapping ideas, I think it'll be a

Marriott tries to defend his 'masterpiece', August 1968.

period. With his wife Jenny Rylands he had moved out of London to a cottage in Essex. And he had also started seeing a lot of a young guitarist that he admired, called Peter Frampton.

The connection had come through a track that Marriott and Lane had produced for The Herd, Frampton's group, called 'Sunshine Cottage'. Marriott, especially, was taken by the young guitarist's ability and, after the mixed reception to 'The Universal', was plainly looking for new avenues to explore.

'I'd written "The Universal" and I honestly thought it was the best song we had at the time,' Marriott explained. 'Ronnie said it was the best single we ever did. I couldn't believe it because at the time I didn't think that he believed in it. I didn't believe anybody believed in it. I thought it was a clever song. The reviews said either it was a stroke of genius or a terrible mistake.

'When it wasn't a hit in a big way it was considered a

mistake and it killed me. I didn't write again for a long while. The disenchantment that comes from even the rest of the guys when things ain't a hit is a crippler. I just went apart in my head.

129

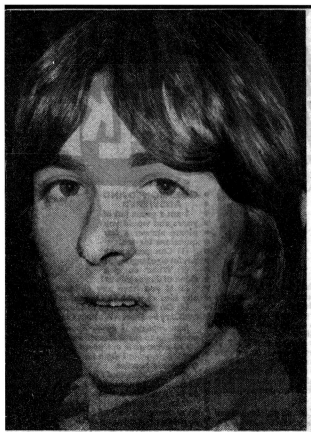

IAN McLAGAN

	JULY 1968					
SUN	MON	TUES	WED	THURS	FRI	SAT
*	1	2	3	4	5	6
7	8	9	10	11	12	13
14	15	16	17	18	19	20
21	22	23	24	25	26	27
28	29	30	31	*	*	*

	AUGUST 1968					
SUN	MON	TUES	WED	THURS	FRI	SAT
*	*	*	*	1	2	3
4	5	6	7	8	9	10
11	12	13	14	15	16	17
18	19	20	21	22	23	24
25	26	27	28	29	30	31

	SEPTEMBER 1968					
SUN	MON	TUES	WED	THURS	FRI	SAT
1	2	3	4	5	6	7
8	9	10	11	12	13	14
15	16	17	18	19	20	21
22	23	24	25	26	27	28
29	30	*	*	*	*	*

'I thought it was a good idea to get Peter Frampton in and have another guitarist, get a fresh start. And he was a very good guitarist, not for what he looked like, a pretty face, which was being put about, but because he was an excellent player. Well, I thought he was.

'He had rung me up and wanted to come over. I think he was a bit of a fan and he wanted advice from me on leaving The Herd, which I couldn't give. None of us were able to give any because we hadn't left a band. I think he just wanted to be in our company.

'He came over and we were playing stuff he had never heard because he was a young boy. We gave him a few joints, he didn't smoke then, and played him a few sounds. I thought he was great. He had a lot of potential as a guitarist. It just seemed a great idea to have another guitarist, change the band a bit, give me a chance to sing properly and maybe get us out of doing that same vein we were still in live since the day we started.

'I mean, the records were different but our stage show hadn't moved forwards at all. So I got him to do some gigs with us. One in Brentwood and a few

more but the others were dead against it. He came to Paris with us and did those tracks with Johnny Hallyday, the French singer who had asked us to be his band. He offered us lots of dough and we did his album and a few TVs. I couldn't even recognise our songs after he had finished with them, they were all changed. One of them was called "Regardez Vous". I thought, that's me, I've written that but I don't know what it's all about. It was sung in French. He sent us all copies and we still get money from it.'

The Small Faces had also worked, with Frampton in tow, on the eponymously titled Skip Bifferty album as well as completing a short tour. But relationships were starting to sour. Ian McLagan, for one, was opposed to Frampton. Not as a person, but because, to coin an Immediate slogan, 'there are but four Small Faces'. Ronnie Lane agreed with him.

'I felt he was an intrusion,' he explained, 'and he was.'

It was while working with Johnny Hallyday that tensions finally erupted. Glyn Johns was organising the sessions.

'I used to produce Hallyday,' he explains, 'and

SMALL FACES want to bring violence back to pop music.

"Pop audiences have changed," explained the very likeable, volatile Steve Marriott. "Once it was screaming all the time when we were on stage, which was great.

"Now they actually sit and listen, which is a bit of a drag.

"There's nothing we like better than a whole crowd of kids rioting, punching bouncers, pulling down walls and hitting each other. It's good for them and it's good for us.

"You see, kids now expect to come and sit and HEAR the sounds on our records—and of course they don't. We can't do it on stage.

"And I hate to disappoint people—but I think we're doing just that on live appearances.

"All these kids have got too sophisticated. Listening to people who think they're cool, telling them they shouldn't be screaming and looning about.

"To be violent on stage is very good for a group. It means that the violent part of our character can be channelled out—and you get a violence buzz back from your audience."

Berserk

What brought about this outburst was Steve's comparison between recent dates the Faces have played in Ireland and Britain.

In Ireland, 5,000 Faces fans went berserk and pushed over a 6 ft wall.

Bring back VIOLENCE!

STEVE MARRIOTT SAYS: WE LOVE KIDS RIOTING AND PUNCHING AND PULLING DOWN WALLS...

ambulance services moved in.

The Small Faces enjoyed all this ferocious display of communication greatly — in fact, they're going back soon to repeat the performance.

"But we've been doing college gigs in Britain and the audiences there are so way above it all. They only like you because you happen to be 'in' at the moment—they don't understand what the hell it's all about.

"And even our own audiences have changed. The kids we more or less grew up with. It's sad."

Small Faces audiences might have changed but they still manage to get the Faces consistently in the chart—which brings us to another point. And that is

record which has caused more hilarity and controversy than any other they've made.

"Actually, it's quite an easy record to suss out," said Steve, and then went into a long rigmarole about why it was—which made it sound twice as complicated. "You have to listen to the words. Not take any notice of the backing and funny noises. And it's no good looking for a story because there isn't one. It's a sentence song.

Smash

"It wasn't done for a single. We wrote it in two hours one morning and recorded the voices on Ronnie's Cassette. The noise of dogs barking was from the garden when our road manager turned up.

"We thought it sounded

No, it wasn't meant to be a send-up of Don Partridge. I wouldn't do that—he's a gas!

"When they decided to put it out we thought—well, either it will be a smash or everyone will hate it. I suppose because of that you could say we're not all that worried about continual chart success. These days anyone can afford to have a flop record as long as their next ones are very good. It isn't the image that counts so much now, it's the record.

"And we're in the position of being able to put out something we like very much ourselves, that satisfies us. If it's a hit—which means the record buying public like it as well—then that's great. If not, at least we're happy."

'Fans actually sit and listen—it's a big drag'

'Temper, temper . . .' Marriott takes on the love 'n' peace brigade, July 1968.

132

Have you ever seen me? The boys surface for air.

he would come to Britain and, basically, whoever was hot at the time in the way of bands, he would try and get them in to make a record with him. I got together The Small Faces and Peter Frampton and we did these sessions in Paris.

'And something happened. I don't know what the argument was about but it had obviously been brewing and this was the last straw. A great argument happened and the shit hit the fan. I was in the

control room and I don't recall what it was about. We went home and the next thing I knew there were two bands.'

In fact it wasn't all over yet. The disgruntled group had been contracted to a New Year's Eve engagement at the Alexandra Palace.

'When we came back from Paris to do Alexandra Palace,' Marriott explained, 'I asked the others if Peter could stay because after France I thought he

133

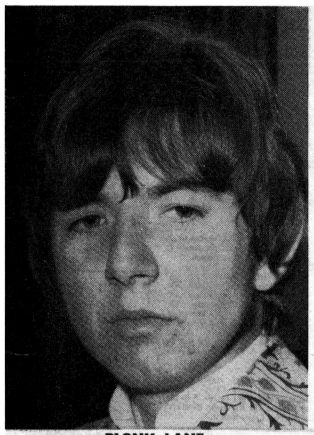

PLONK LANE

OCTOBER 1968						
SUN	MON	TUES	WED	THURS	FRI	SAT
*	*	1	2	3	4	5
6	7	8	9	10	11	12
13	14	15	16	17	18	19
20	21	22	23	24	25	26
27	28	29	30	31	*	*

NOVEMBER 1968						
SUN	MON	TUES	WED	THURS	FRI	SAT
*	*	*	*	*	1	2
3	4	5	6	7	8	9
10	11	12	13	14	15	16
17	18	19	20	21	22	23
24	25	26	27	28	29	30

DECEMBER 1968						
SUN	MON	TUES	WED	THURS	FRI	SAT
1	2	3	4	5	6	7
8	9	10	11	12	13	14
15	16	17	18	19	20	21
22	23	24	25	26	27	28
29	30	31	*	*	*	*

made a great improvement on the band. Another influence, another player and someone I could do dual things with.

'Anyway, they all hated it and that was a big downer and the gig was so bad. It was horrendously bad. No one was looking at each other, it was a shambles really. Alexis Korner got up to play. It was my idea, I must admit, but I didn't think it was going to be that much of a shambles.

'I thought, this is terrible. I slung my guitar down and did a very unprofessional thing, and just walked off. It wasn't even finished. I just thought, this is horrible.'

'Steve,' Kenney Jones remembers, 'went on stage that night in a very bad mood and we knew something was up. He had been throwing real wobblers all week and then halfway through the set he just threw his guitar down and walked off, leaving us like three lemons.

'We looked at each other and it was like, "Well, see ya." There was this almighty scream up afterwards, especially Mac. He went mad, but Steve just simply said he couldn't do it any more. He felt we couldn't cross over from being a pop band into heavier music. He felt it was too difficult, which was wrong because we really had it all and were going that way naturally.

'I'll always remember when it was announced in the papers. It said, "Steve quits to play with better musicians," which broke my heart because I always thought we were all right.'

According to Marriott, the band's studio progress had not been matched by their live work. On record

'I went through that scene where everything went wrong for me. It was a drag, man. I tried too hard. I listened to so much advice that I wondered who I was. I was told what to do for my public image and if I wasn't careful I started believing in the image and forgetting about myself.'

STEVE MARRIOTT, OCTOBER 1968

they had artistically kept on the move, refusing to stick to one sound. Live, the reverse was true. And relationships had now passed breaking point. Lane was no longer speaking to Marriott, though

'Imagine if you had a record and you played it every night on stage for three years. Then you get some idea of the sort of feelings that we have about "Sha La La La Lee" and "Lazy Sunday" and the rest.'

STEVE MARRIOTT, JUNE 1969

McLagan was. He made one last attempt to talk Marriott round, but to no avail: 'Steve told me that he felt after "Lazy Sunday" and those kind of songs that The Small Faces were becoming to him a joke

'I've changed in myself and the group has changed as things have happened to us. In the days of "All Or Nothing" we were a moody pop group. Then "Lazy Sunday" showed us as a group that likes to enjoy themselves. It's very funny when you think about the past. We used to be really aggressive and, of course, we still are on stage. But on record, with "Lazy Sunday" and Ogdens' Nut Gone, we are turning into a funny group, because basically we are a comical group. I think this came across, especially on the album.'

STEVE MARRIOTT, SEPTEMBER 1968

band and he didn't want that. He thought it was best that he left and give us some fresh air.'

There was also another factor at play, which both Marriott and Lane later conceded: Marriott felt he couldn't top the huge success of Ogdens' within the framework of The Small Faces. His insecurity on the matter had obviously taken him over and dictated that he quit while on top.

'After the last album the next one has got to be better. The last one was a rather contrived, metallic thing born out of living in the city. Living out here we are writing more country music with bottle neck and lots of acoustic guitar.'

STEVE MARRIOTT, JANUARY 1969

It should also be noted that the band had by now reached their mid-twenties. They had been together, literally day and night, for too many years. They were all growing up and changing as people. Marriott felt he had to follow a musical path that his recent material, such as the early heavy metal sound of 'Wham

The end is approaching but you'd never know from this close-knit shot, circa 1968.

'We all lived together and the whole thing was based on togetherness. Obviously, there had to be a reaction. It was so ironic. There we were beginning to hate the sight of each other and all our publicity was based on our togetherness. We rowed constantly over niggly little things and in the end we decided to cool it for a while. Now, of course, we don't see each other nearly so often and our friendships are more the stronger for it. As long as we are together there will be rumours we are splitting up.'

STEVE MARRIOTT, OCTOBER 1968

Bam Thank You Mam', was now dictating to him. He wanted to make music that had even more depth to it and he no doubt believed that that was impossible within The Small Faces line-up. That aside, he still felt enough for the band to end it with dignity and not prolong it as a money-making but painful operation. Even at the end principles still mattered.

'Steve got frightened by many things,' Lane says. 'He was insecure about his talent although I don't see why he should be. If anyone had a whole lot of

Steve is an Elf. Why? Because he is artistic and likes feasts and orgies...

TONY NORMAN reporting

LITTLE CHILDREN are frightened of the dark; old ladies are frightened of putting on weight; and over the last couple of years pop journalists have been frightened of the Small Faces.

So, when photographer Chris Walter and I ventured out into the fair countryside of Essex, as the first journalistic team to visit Steve Marriot in his new home, we nervously wondered what lay ahead.

Licking

After receiving directions from a dustman who sounded as if he'd been educated at Cambridge (really!), we came across the beautiful white-walled, thatched cottage.

I slowly swung open the front gate, on which was printed the name of the cottage (a sworn secret!), and was leapt upon by three hairy individuals!

No, not Ronnie, Mac and Kenny—it was Steve's three pet dogs, Lucy, Love and Seamus.

After much licking and tail-wagging I jumped to my feet and followed the dogs to their Master.

Steve was sitting upstairs tucking into an enormous plate full of sausages, eggs, chips and tomatoes.

Then it happened!

Steve threw something at us. It was the warmest smile of greeting you could ever wish for, and for the next two hours we were treated to the kindest hospitality I have ever received in my career as a journalist.

I asked him to tell me all about his new home.

Shared

"Well, my lawyer told me to buy a house, while I still had the bread," explained Steve.

"I've been looking for a proper home for two years now, but this was worth waiting for.

"Ronnie and I shared the cost of £15,000 and he is working on what used to be the stables in days gone by. He's got some fantastic ideas for the place.

"Jenny and I have this three-bedroomed cottage and both buildings stand in an area of three acres.

"We've been here for three weeks now and we love it!

"I find it very easy to work down here and since I arrived I've got more material together than during six months in London."

Steve pushed aside his half-eaten lunch, because it was getting "soggy", and we turned to the subject of the Faces' latest record.

"We didn't want Universal put out as a single, but when we raised our objections we were told 30,000 had already been printed.

"It would have made a beautiful L.P. track but as a single it was destined to be a 'limbo record', just touching the Twenty.

"If my mother can't understand a record, then I know it's not commercial!"

Suddenly, he leapt to his feet and laughed. "Hey, come and watch Marriot the Miner!"

We strolled downstairs into the garden, and while Steve filled the coal bucket I noticed a couple of ducks waddling around.

Copper

"Oh, they come from the stream along the bottom of the garden. There's a beautiful waterfall there, which makes a lovely, fresh, relaxing sound in the evenings."

What with dogs, cats and ducks, Steve had his own mini-zoo, I suggested.

"Yes, I guess I have," laughed Steve. "I love animals and the way they all mix together.

"They mix so much better than humans. I mean could you imagine me living happily with a vicar and a copper? Ridiculous!"

I commented that this large garden was going to take a lot of looking after.

"Yes, that's right," he agreed. "You'll never believe this, but I'm taking gardening lessons from a guy who comes in every Friday. I'm not very good yet, but at least I'm keen."

Next, this new, domesticated Small Face led us proudly into his beautiful ground floor lounge.

Thick fur rugs covered the floors, a pistol hung on a wall and the coal fire seemed to fill the room with a warm glow of happiness and security.

"Jenny designed this room just how she wanted it. I left it to her, because this is to be her home and I want more than anything else in the world, for her to be happy here," said Steve quietly.

Like any young man in love, Steve Marriot is a very happy, contented person.

However, he soon showed a flash of anger when I asked him if he would ever go back to Australia, after the treatment they received on their last visit.

"Yes, we will be going back to Australia," he replied.

"Last time it took us three weeks to build up the kind of reputation it took the Stones four years to build here, and we were good boys.

"This time we won't behave and see what happens," he said in a voice that would have made a kangeroo have kittens!

Despair

And the storm subsided . . .

"We won't be playing in Britain again for some time," he continued. "I think we have played at every ballroom in Britain at least three times, and the kids must be getting tired of it.

"We are turning to new markets, and hope to come to grips with both Germany and Sweden which we will be visiting."

Did Steve share the despair that many people are feeling about pop music today?

"No, because I feel that musically and artistically, the scene is better than ever.

"We have excellent new groups like Spooky Tooth and the Nice coming along, which can't be bad.

"However, I do find myself feeling sorry for groups like the Herd, especially for poor little Peter Frampton, because of the tremendous pressure they are under.

"All the Small Faces live in the country now and we are so relaxed. We have found peace of mind.

"We hope to build our own recording studio here in the grounds of the cottage and hope eventually to have our own record label, so we will have complete freedom of choice of material.

"We would probably record other artistes, but that worries me because we would become business men, and I don't want that.

Smashed

"I hate that word 'business'. It's like a game of draughts where you must eliminate others to succeed," he said, a troubled frown crossing his brow.

Still, yours truly soon had him laughing again!

As I leapt to my feet to say goodbye, I smashed my head on one of the beams which run across the ceiling of the 300-year-old lounge.

"Hey you're a giant person, and this house belongs to Elf people!" laughed Steve.

Well, maybe it's just me but when someone says something like that out of the blue, I feel I must ask them to explain!

"Oh it's something we've been reading about which says we all originated from things like Wolves, Goblins and Elves.

"Elf people like feasts and orgies and are artistic, so that's what I am!" he smiled.

"Anyway, it's a nice thing to believe in," he added "nicer than Christianity."

Barks, quacks, me-ows smiles, warm handshakes and all too soon we were waving goodbye to our kind host.

And the contented "Elf Of Epping Forest" and his beautiful princess lived happily ever after . . .

'Anyway, it's a nice thing to believe in... better than Christianity'

Marriot moves to the country.

'People are more interested in music now than in images which is great and all we want to do is get better musically and stay together. We'd have broken up a long while ago if we didn't want to work as mates and improve.'

STEVE MARRIOTT, JANUARY 1968

talent it was him. As for that gig, I was pissed off. I thought it was very unprofessional.'

The Alexandra Palace appearance was not the group's final show. In January, they were contracted to tour Germany.

'That,' said McLagan, 'was the only time we made any money playing live and that was because I took over the finances. Everybody was ripping us off but once I took care of the cash we made some money. As for the tour, I don't remember it being strained or anything.'

When they returned to the UK the group was effectively over although for now the public was kept in the dark. If anyone harboured any thoughts of the band surviving, they were fooling themselves. Relationships had broken down and Marriott and the group barely spoke for years afterwards. Neither side could understand the other.

'We just feel that old scene as The Small Faces had become a bit stagnant and we want to feel that we can be free to develop.'

RONNIE LANE, FEBRUARY 1969

'Ronnie,' Marriott recalled, 'lived in this barn at the back of me which made it embarrassing. I had this little cottage and there was another cottage at the back of it on the same land, like a barn, and Ronnie lived in that.

'He was moving out but it took about

'There was no friction between us. In fact I still see Steve quite a bit. It was just that he wanted to go and do something different. Steve was a powerful influence in The Faces. But his going has given the rest of us a chance to come on stronger.'

RONNIE LANE, JUNE 1969

three months, which was awful because there was all this bad feeling which there needn't have been, to be honest. I talked to him afterwards about it all and he couldn't understand why I had to go. I wasn't getting the vibes and the band wasn't playing well.

'Years later, after Ron left The Faces, he finally knew and he said to me, "I now know how you felt but I didn't at the time." You can't, you see, because dissatisfaction is for the individual.'

In early 1969, rumours of the split circulated in the music press until March 1969 when an official announcement finally laid the band to rest. On 7 March 'Afterglow'/'Wham Bam Thank You Mam' was put out by Immediate. It reached thirty-six. The following November they also issued a double album, *The Autumn Stone*, comprising three live tracks taken from Newcastle City Hall, various hit

Immediate advert for 'Afterglow' playing on the rumours of a split.

The tensions become public. Finally.

Small Faces talk about Group split

SMALL FACES in more peaceful times (l to r) KENNY JONES, "PLONK" LANE, IAN McLAGAN and STEVE MARRIOTT.

MONTHS of speculation about the future of the Small Faces ended this week when lead singer Steve Marriott broke his silence to tell NME, "The group is definitely breaking up."

Rumours that Steve was about to leave the group have been sweeping the pop world, but from the seclusion of his Essex country cottage he said, "I want to make it clear that it's not a case of my leaving the group but rather that the group is breaking up to pursue their own scenes."

During their four years together the Small Faces have been one of the country's most popular and commercially successful groups and Steve admits:

"Of course it's sad in some ways that it's all over but it's great for each of us to have the chance to do what we really want to. And we had to get away from being labelled a dirty pop group for 'teen screams. That wasn't what we wanted at all but while the group stayed together as it was it was an image we were stuck with."

The most favoured story in current circulation is that Steve will team up in a new group with close friend and ex-Herd lead singer Peter Frampton but his only reply to the rumours was a guarded: "At this stage I'd rather not comment on my future plans.

"The name 'Small Faces' has become a bit of a hang-up. It no longer means what we originally intended it to mean and the only thing we can do is to get rid of it," Steve told me bluntly.

"All our plans are a bit vague at the moment and no date has been set, but we all intend to stay in the pop music business. But I will say that we hope that two good things can come out of one good thing."

Ronnie "Plonk" Lane, Faces' lead guitarist, said that the proposed demob of the group was not because of any personal disagreement amongst the boys.

"We just feel that old scene as the Small Faces has become a bit stagnant and we want to feel that we can be free to develop," he said.

When I asked the two other boys what their plans were, Kenny Jones said that his one great purpose in life was to become a really good drummer.

"I have been doing a lot of session work just lately and I intend to go on with this for the time being," he said.

Until now silent, organist Ian McLagan—with a cheeky grin on his face—chipped in: "My one great ambition in life is to play the organ in Westminster Cathedral!"

Final word about the split came from Steve. "Imagine if you had a record and you played it every night on stage for three years. Then you get some idea about the sort of feelings that we have about "Sha La La La Lee" and "Lazy Sunday" and the rest."

singles and studio cuts and, perhaps, in the title track, one of Marriott's finest songs.

'The group is definitely breaking up. I want to make it clear that it's not a case of my leaving the group but rather that the group is breaking up to pursue its own scenes. Of course it's sad in some ways that it's all over but it's great for each of us to have the chance to do what we really want to do. And we had to get away from being labelled a dirty pop group for teen screams.'

STEVE MARRIOTT, FEBRUARY 1969

'The Autumn Stone' is a beautiful and timeless acoustic ballad filled with Marriott's heartfelt vocals and reflective lyrics. Just as important is the sensitive backing it receives from his increasingly estranged companions, a far cry from the energetic and raucous spirit that informed so much of their work. The song's full and languid production coupled with its musical depth, previews a very mature sensibility at work.

'Yesterday is gone but not my memories,' Marriott sings. Though the song is ostensibly addressing a lover, the singer could well have been thinking about the group he was about to leave. Despite the broken friendships, the tensions and the grievances,

Marriott's memory of The Small Faces would always be positive. Indeed, once time had healed the wounds, all would look back with increasing pride at the music they had created and the deep friendships that had seen them through the crazy times.

Also of interest on this album are the live cuts, especially the full rendition of 'Every Little Bit Hurts'. Just towards the song's end, after an impassioned Marriott vocal, the band break down the song and Marriott asks the audience to join in on the chorus. He is met by a barrage of screams. In that one moment, The Small Faces's relationship with their live audience is brilliantly crystallised.

That the public's interest in the band had waned can be gauged by the album's poor sales and non-existent chart placing. With the band bickering in public, aligned with a general feeling that *The Autumn Stone* was not a true album, Small Faces fans simply lost interest. Immediate by now were also heading for disaster and did not have the funds to promote the LP. It seemed the album had arrived too late to make a significant impact.

'The Autumn Stone* wasn't a legitimate album,' Marriott stated, 'it was Andrew's put together. By then I'd already left The Small Faces. The last complete thing we did together was the song "The Autumn Stone", which was going to be the title track of the next Small Faces album, and "Wham Bam Thank You Mam". Those two tracks were supposed to be a single but Andrew didn't like "The Autumn Stone" [Andrew replaced "Stone" on the A-side with "Afterglow" from *Ogdens'*]. The irony is he wound up using it as the title for the album.

'We'd recorded a lot of tracks which we never had a chance to finish. They had titles just to mark the tape boxes with – "Colibosher", "Wide Eyed Girl On The Wall" – and they were thrown in as instrumentals. *The Autumn Stone*'s three live tracks were from Newcastle City Hall just after *Ogdens'* came out. We'd thought about a live album and wanted to see what it was like.

'I don't remember too well but I think they recorded a couple of sets – with and without the horn section which appears on three tracks – at a couple of gigs that were real scream machines. It

No split with Small Faces: new man is signed

SMALL FACES will **NOT** split again! A replacement has been found for Steve Marriott, who quit to form a new group some months ago, and Ronnie Lane, Kenny Jones and Ian MacLaglan seem set to stay together for both records and "live" appearances.

Disc learned on Tuesday that after weeks of indecision the Faces had agreed to remain as a group—and had engaged a new guitarist. At the moment his name is being kept a close secret, but he has been busy working and rehearsing with the others for some weeks.

A likely candidate may be Ron Wood, guitarist with the Jeff Beck Group, who has spent a lot of time with the Faces recently.

A close friend of the Faces told Disc: "As far as I know, Ron is definitely joining the Faces. He's been practising with them a lot. But there may be hang-ups over contracts."

● Steve Marriott meanwhile, who quit the Faces to form a new group, Humble Pie, with ex-Herd man Peter Frampton, returned from holiday last weekend. A debut album is set for early July.

Who will complete the Kenny Jones, Ronnie Lane, Ian MacLaglan Small Faces line up?

The Faces start to take shape.

was done on a four-track with Glyn Johns at the knobs.

'At first, Andrew wanted use of the stuff for The Small Faces, who were going to continue without me, and Ronnie wanted me to help mix the stuff, so I did. There's probably more of it sitting round somewhere.'

The Small Faces were not the only ones to self-implode around this time. Immediate, their management and label company, followed suit about a year after the group's demise. Their policy of picking up hits from America and issuing them in Britain had not yielded massive financial gain. Their own British signings, especially The Small

'We've recorded at my studios at my house. Ronnie asked me to play lead guitar for them as a favour. They don't quite know what's happening. They were making the discs to see how things would work out without Steve. Although Ronnie's voice lacks Steve's projection, they still sound very like The Small Faces.'

PETE TOWNSHEND, FEBRUARY 1969

Faces, had been allowed countless expensive hours in studios without any check on the money that was being spent. As soon as the money rolled in it rolled out again, despite their impressive track

141

Herd: don't rely on the past

The troubled triangle involving the Herd, Small Faces and Humble Pie is on its way to settlement — DISC has a look

Face: it's bee a bit toug

AS the turmoils continue in the troubled camps of the Small Faces and Humble Pie, the new-look Herd trio carry on as normal, and are enjoying a new high in morale for the first time in months.

First there was the upset of Peter Frampton leaving, thought by some to herald the end of the group; then, just as the three remaining members had got themselves sorted out and made a new single "The Game" came the tragic news of drummer Andrew Steel's illness. Doctors told him he must immediately rest, and under no circumstances should he ever play drums again.

Two setbacks in a row, which, coupled with the fact that no-one seems to have wanted to play that new single, you would have thought would have ended the Herd once and for all.

Not so—and now, complete with new drummer Henry Spinetti, zany younger brother of comedian/actor/writer Victor, the Herd are confidently picking up the threads, covering up the traces and forging ahead.

"Despite all we're still working quite well, in ballrooms, and we're very pleased and often surprised by the good reaction we've been getting," says Andy Bown.

"We don't play the Herd's old hits any more, partly because we never could play them very well on stage anyway, especially 'Paradise Lost,' and partly because we don't really want to rely on the past for our success."

Despite being only a three-some, the Herd continue to display their musical versatility. Andy fluctuates between his much-prized "flash" Hammond B-3 organ, lead guitar and bass guitar; Gary plays lead and bass guitar; and Henry plays drums and pulls funny faces!

Andy is naturally disappointed at the apparent reluctance of Radio 1 to play their first "Frampton-less" single "The Game." He still feels that with the airplay it could have made the Top Twenty.

"But we're already working on another single which I think is even more commercial than 'The Game,' and as we do quite definitely need a hit record we'll be going all out on that!"

Andy's also hoping to take advantage of Brian Auger's return to England.

"Before they had the hit with 'Wheels On Fire' he promised to give me some tuition in how to play the organ properly. I'm a terrible player, even though I reckon I'm probably better than 75 per cent!"

Humble Pie: equality!

HUMBLE PIE hits the public ear at the end of this month. Their first album is released at the end of this month called — naturally—"Humble Pie" and is a form of every kind of music from C-n-W and folk to "heavy" instrumental.

Humble Pie, in case you don't know, is what happened to Peter Frampton and Steve Marriott. From what one can surmise the general feeling about this new group is that they will be very far from humble. But the idea is that whereas Frampton and Marriott, when they were with groups, were the "stars," each member of "Humble Pie" will breathe equality at us. It will be interesting to see if this theory works in practice.

Their first plans are to appear at special free concerts in London —forerunner to all this being dates on the Continent. And after that? Well, America for a start.

And so a new group is once again formed from the debris of another of pop's personality explosions. But where did it all start?

Once Peter Frampton was described as the "Face Of '68"—and at the time it suited him.

Clean-cut, good-looking, sweetly boyish on the outside he exemplified pop music faces last year.

But times change and so do people, and suddenly Peter Frampton shocked everyone who saw him as a lead singer without a thought in his head but his own looks and the screaming they roused when he came on stage. He calmly walked away from the Herd and almost disappeared.

It turned out that what he was actually doing was getting over a year's hard, exhausting work with the Herd, and "getting it together" with Steve Marriott in the country.

Humble Pie — not so humble

So off went Peter and Steve, recently dissociated from the Small Faces, thought by some in the scene despite how hands were raised in astonishment at their tie-up.

Both had left groups at a time when success and fame was three-fold upon their heads. Both felt that what they were doing wasn't what they wanted to do. Both were frustrated, tired, and not all that placid. Both saw music as a lot more than they could achieve within the confines of the groups they were with.

To solve all these problems the only way out was to start all over again.

Frampton had always had a frustrated desire to get to grips with a guitar and become much more than just a face and a pretty singer. He and Marriott found Jerry Shirley and Greg Ridley (ex-Spooky Tooth) were both sympathetic to the ideas of a new group.

Certainly the innovation of any new group — specially one with a history like Humble Pie's — is welcome. They have all moved a long way from the "teenybopper" audience where they were born. So far Humble Pie is still in its infancy. Whether they are going to contribute to music more than we've heard to date is something we'll have to wait to decide until next month.

Small Faces: hoping

THE Small Faces, fans will be relieved to learn, are alive and well . . . and living in HOPE! Hope that before very long they will be rid of the business problems which have beset their little lives since Steve Marriott quit their ranks.

"We'll be glad to get back on the scene again," revealed Ronnie "Plonk" Laine. "We've had enough hang-ups lately to last a lifetime. All we want to do is write and sing and play."

The Faces — Ronnie, Kenny Jones and Ian MacLaglan — slipped from the pop spotlight earlier this year when leader Steve Marriott confirmed long-standing rumours that he was splitting to team up with Herd star Peter Frampton.

"There was no friction between us," explained Ronnie. "In fact, I still see Steve quite a bit. It was just that he wanted to go and do something different."

And the publicity and controversy which followed the proposed formation of the new so-called "supergroup" Humble Pie left the remaining Faces in something of a quandary. The future looked more than bleak. Steve Marriott had undoubtedly been one of the group's mainstays. He was also a powerful songwriter responsible for many of their hits.

Over to "Plonk," currently resident house-guest at the Twickenham riverside home of his friend, Pete Townshend: "Steve was a powerful influence in the Faces. But his going has given the rest of us a chance to come on stronger. Even if it has been a bit tough."

He explained: "We're not exactly broke. But it's been a bit of a job making ends meet. We've been writing and rehearsing a lot, but haven't been in the recording studios for nine months. And we've only done a few 'live' gigs."

In fact, during the period when the three Faces were unsure of their future — at times there was talk of a total break-up — drummer Kenny Jones was moved to work as a session musician to make ends meet.

"Plonk" grinned his impish grin. "It sounds bad, doesn't it? But we'll be OK, you see. What's happened to us over the past few months has rather destroyed my faith in some people. But it's made me a lot shrewder.

"I'm personally just as happy now as I was when it was all happening for us. It's just that I' more frustrated!"

First move towards the b comeback has been the signing well almost! — of a permanent r placement for Steve Marriott. F is, as exclusively revealed in la week's Disc, Ron Wood, current guitarist with Jeff Beck.

Says "Plonk": "He's been wor ing with us a lot lately. He'll jo as soon as contract problems a cleared up."

Small Faces may also chan; their name. And by ditching the title hope to be able to make completely fresh start.

"Kenny wants to keep the nan because we had a lot of ha work building it up. But M wants to change it. Me? I'm eas I don't mind. It's really only shop-front through which you s your goods."

And after talking to "Plonl it's obvious that the Faces' ne future is definitely rosy. They ha plenty of first-class goods to se

'Andrew liked to live lavishly,' Marriott also pointed out. 'He was the first one to have one of those big Rollers with black windows. He couldn't really afford it, the thing was on a mortgage.

'Immediate had a string of big hits all in a row, each one that came out was a big hit. But then they stopped. They took a load of hacks, like John Mayall and Jimmy Page, and spent a load of money on them and they didn't do anything. They put everything they had into them and I don't think what came back was enough to save the company.

'Andrew was great about it, though. He just said, "We're going under, mates." He warned us all. He said, "Get out now and sort yourselves out. Get other labels because I don't want any of you going down with the company." He was a great bloke, a right old blagger, but underneath all the front he was a very nice man.

'As for me, I couldn't see how we could follow Ogdens'. It was a worldwide hit [except for the US] that wasn't really a true picture of us

Line-ups are resolved, but they won't talk for years.

record of producing intriguing pop records for the masses.

live. We tried to do some of it live and it sounded awful . . . Whatever you read in print, it was in fact a case of "Marriott was scared."'

The Small Faces, so often viewed as the jokers in the pack, had fallen apart in anger and tears. As Marriott once told me, they had started off laughing at the world and now it was laughing back at them. All four members were broke when the split occurred. Marriott was out on his own and it would take many years for the wounds to heal properly.

Meanwhile, the quality of The Small Faces' work would remain a secret for many years. One reason for this was that the writers who came to commentate about the sixties only examined the obvious. For them, it was always The Beatles, The Rolling Stones, Dylan and, maybe, The Who that defined the era. In their books and photographic collections, The Small Faces are never mentioned or depicted. Against the mass popularity of the likes of McCartney, Jagger, Lennon and Richards, they simply disappear. That is not to put the aforementioned acts down – their influence and strength are undeniable. But such a reading, by ignoring the deeper truths, perfectly explains why so many greats are consigned to the sidelines and eventual obscurity. There is also a whiff of class snobbery here, a feeling that four boisterous lads from the East End could never have reached the heights they did.

And yet, in a cruel twist of irony, it is somehow fitting that The Small Faces received such a treatment – in true Mod philosophy, it is always the hidden jewels that carry the most riches.

Life's a drag.

Steve Marriott, circa 1987.

AFTERGLOW OF YOUR LOVE

STEVE MARRIOTT

After quitting The Small Faces, Stephen Peter Marriott formed Humble Pie with Peter Frampton (vocals/guitar), Jerry Shirley (drums) and Greg Ridley (bass). Three years later, Frampton left and was replaced by Dave Clempson (guitar). The band made nine albums, the first two for Immediate, before it crashed, and the remainder for A&M Records. The group split up in 1975.

Marriott's next venture was The Steve Marriott All Stars with Mickey Finn (guitar), Dave Clempson (guitar), Ian Wallace (drums) and Greg Ridley (bass). They lasted a year but did not issue any records.

In 1976 Marriott cut a solo album, *Marriott*, for A&M. On one side he used all British musicians, including Ridley and Clempson, and on the flip side he used only American musicians.

A year later, Marriott returned to Britain to take part in a Small Faces reunion. 'Itchycoo Park' had been re-released and had reached the top ten, thus creating the impetus for the band's reformation. The rest of the line-up was Kenney Jones

(drums), Ian McLagan (keyboards) and Rick Wills (bass). Ronnie Lane had attended early rehearsals but decided not to participate. The next year, Jimmy McCulloch (guitar) was added to the line-up.

The reformed Small Faces cut two albums for Atlantic, *Playmates* (1977) and *78 In The Shade* (1978). Soon after, they disbanded.

In 1980, Marriott reformed Humble Pie with Jerry Shirley (drums) and Anthony Jones (bass). They cut one album, *On To Victory*, before expanding the line-up to include Bobby Tench (guitar) and Clem Clempson (guitar).

Another album, *Go For The Throat*, was issued before Marriott called it a day and returned to Britain. He then formed a succession of pub groups, such as Steve Marriott and the Packet of Three, Steve Marriott and the Official Receivers and Steve Marriott and the DTs.

In February 1991, he flew out to Los Angeles and recorded four tracks with Peter Frampton. Two months later, on 20 April, he returned home to his cottage in Saffron Walden, Essex. Some time during the night a fire broke out. Marriott was unable to escape from the flames. His body was found the next day.

A funeral service, attended by hundreds of well-wishers, including Kenney Jones, Peter Frampton and Joe Brown, was held two weeks later in a crematorium at Saffron Walden. His parents donated an inscribed bench in commemoration of their son's life. It now sits in the grounds of the crematorium.

RONNIE LANE

Ronald Frederick Lane continued working with Ian McLagan and Kenney Jones. In June 1969, after months of free rehearsal time at The Stones's Bermondsey studio, they launched The Faces, along with ex-Jeff Beck bassist Ron Wood on guitar and Rod Stewart on vocals.

The group released seven singles and four studio albums, *First Step*, *Long Players*, *A Nod's As Good As A Wink To A Blind Horse* and *Ooh La La* (on Warner Brothers), as well as a live album, *Coast To Coast: Overtures and Beginners*.

Lane appeared on all of the above apart from the live album and the band's final single, 'You Can Make Me Dance, Sing or Anything'. In 1973 he left the group to form his own band Slim Chance with Benny Gallagher and Graham Lyle (guitar, accordion). Lane's position in The Faces was taken by Tetsu Yamauchi.

Slim Chance's line-up was augmented by Chris Stewart (bass), Kevin Westlake (guitar), Jimmy Jewel (sax), Bruce Rowland (drums) and Billy Livesey (piano) with Lane on vocals and guitar.

The band's first single, 'How Come', reached number eleven in the charts. Encouraged by this early success, Lane put together The Passing Show tour which incorporated the Chipperfields's Circus Big Top, along with their acts and staff. The band travelled around the UK performing in towns and villages not normally visited by groups. An album, *Anymore For Anymore*, was also released.

After eight weeks of poorly attended shows, the tour collapsed. Undeterred, Lane returned to the studio and cut 'The Poacher', which reached the UK top ten. He also bought the first ever mobile recording studio which was built into the shell of an airstream caravan.

In 1974 the original line-up drifted away through lack of money and Lane reformed the group with Ruan O'Lochlainn (keys, guitar, saxophone), Brian Belshaw (bass), Charley Hart (fiddle, accordion, sax, keys), Glen Le Fleur (drums) and Steve Simpson (fiddle, mandolin, guitar, harmonica), who had played fiddle on 'How Come'.

Over the next two years, the group toured England and Scandinavia and released two albums, *Slim Chance* and *One For The Road*, both of which scraped into the top forty. Once again, lack of money forced the group apart.

In 1976 Lane opted to concentrate on a solo career and running his mobile studio. Musicians who used the studio included The Who, for their *Quadrophenia* album, and Eric Clapton for his live comeback LP, recorded that year at The Royal Albert Hall.

Unfortunately, the financial and legal problems surrounding the collapse of Slim Chance resulted in Lane being declared bankrupt. At the same time it was discovered that he had contracted multiple sclerosis, an illness from which his mother also suffered.

It was at this time that Pete Townshend persuaded Lane to leave his Welsh farm and come to London to record an album with him. The resulting LP, *Rough Mix* (with The Stones's Charlie Watts on drums), received critical acclaim and healthy sales.

Lane then attempted controversial MS cures in America but returned to England with no noticeable results. He moved into a flat in east London, taking his mobile studio with him. Unfortunately, local vandals wrecked the vehicle and Lane had only insured the mobile's wiring, not the equipment inside.

His next project was The Ronnie Lane Band (sometimes named Ronnie Lane's Big Dipper) which played low-key gigs and support slots. About this time he met fellow MS sufferer ex-model Vivian Neves and involved himself in ARMS (Action Research Into Multiple Sclerosis).

Offers from members of The Rolling Stones, The Who, Jimmy Page, Jeff Beck, Steve Winwood, Andy Fairweather Low and Kenney Jones resulted in a charity show at London's Royal Albert Hall, under the production of Glyn Johns. The gig raised a staggering £100,000. Lane then returned to America to set up ARMS USA which, over the next few years, he funded through similar concerts and tours. Unfortunately, legal and financial problems saw the office of ARMS USA closed down by the mid-eighties.

In 1986 Rod Stewart invited all The Faces to join him for twenty minutes at the end of one of his Wembley shows. Bill Wyman played bass and Ronnie Lane appeared on stage in a wheelchair.

Lane returned to America and settled in Austin,

Texas. The town honoured his arrival by staging a Ronnie Lane Day. In 1988, Lane hired a Texan group, The Tremors, to back him on a short tour of the States. The band was also assisted by Rolling Stones saxophonist, Bobby Keyes.

The concerts were attended by such luminaries as Kris Kristofferson, The Stray Cats, Mick Taylor and Bruce Springsteen. Unfortunately, Lane's condition deteriorated further, making touring an impossibility, apart from a last outing to Japan in 1991, when he was accompanied by various Tremors members and Ian McLagan.

Ronnie Lane still lives in Austin, Texas, and is currently planning a new album.

KENNEY JONES

After the demise of The Faces in 1975, Kenneth Thomas Jones was asked by Rod Stewart to join his band. Jones accepted but on the day of his flight to America had a sudden change of heart. He pulled his drums off the plane and went home.

In 1976, as an experiment, Jones cut a solo single entitled 'Ready Or Not'/'Woman Trouble'. He then went into session work. Albums he has appeared on include two Joan Armatrading albums, *Joan Armatrading* and *Show Some Emotion*, Andy Fairweather Low's *La Booga Rooga* and The Rolling Stones's hit single 'It's Only Rock 'n' Roll.

In 1980, following Keith Moon's death, he was invited to join The Who. He has since left the group and is currently negotiating a Faces comeback tour.

IAN McLAGAN

Since The Small Faces reunion and subsequent demise, Ian Patrick McLagan has not joined any groups. Rather, he has spent his time making guest appearances on record for acts as disparate as The Rich Kids (formed by ex-Sex Pistols bassist Glen Matlock), Bruce Springsteen, Buddy Guy, Tammy Wynette, The Rolling Stones (on their hit single 'Miss You'), The Everly Brothers and Bob Dylan.

Apart from various Faces reunions, he has also appeared on stage with The New Barbarians, a loose collection of musicians put together by Keith Richards, featuring, among others, his old Faces cohort Ron Wood, Jackson Browne and, most recently, Paul Weller.

When he has some free time on his hands, he often plays small clubs in his adopted hometown of Los Angeles.

In 1993 Ian McLagan accompanied Rod Stewart on his American tour following the huge success of Stewart's *Unplugged . . . and Seated* album and is currently involved in tentative discussions surrounding the proposed reformation of The Faces.

Ronnie, Kenney and Ian while in The Faces, circa 1973.

Music and animals were Marriott's main loves.

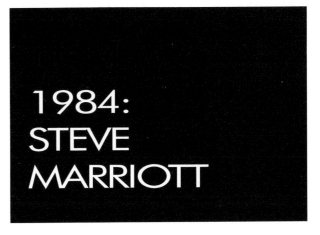

1984:
STEVE
MARRIOTT

I n early December 1984, I was assigned by the *New Musical Express* to interview Steve Marriott. His new group, The Packet of Three, had a live album scheduled for release and Marriott was out and about on the promotional see-saw.

Having some knowledge of his musical background (he and I part company with the formation of Humble Pie), I arranged to meet him in The Small Faces's old West End hangout, the Giaconda café in Denmark Street. I was hoping that the location would trigger his memory and bring out stories he may have forgotten about himself and the group.

I arrived at about three-thirty, fifteen minutes behind schedule. Marriott was sitting impatiently at a table, drumming his fingers. He wore a large overcoat and a cap. His face was full and he sported a small moustache. After the introductions, we sat chatting for about a minute or two. I can't remember what we were talking about but he suddenly asked, 'Do we have to stay here? There's a little boozer I know we can go to. It depresses me too much being in here.'

This was before the pubs were allowed to open all day so I had no idea where he was intending to go.

'Sure,' I replied, 'if that's what you want.'

We left the Giaconda and Marriott took me next door to the Tin Pan Alley Club, a members-only drinking club. It was a haunt he knew well from the old days.

'Right,' he said. 'What are you having?'

I am a terrible afternoon drinker, but I figured that if my subject was going for it I should put such considerations aside and brave the storm.

'I'll have a vodka and tonic, thanks,' I told him.

'Good, I'll have a double whiskey and Coke and don't complain because I know you get expenses from the *NME*, so get up to the bar.'

You can only applaud cheek like that.

Marriott and I had a couple of rounds but the noise inside the club made an interview impossible. We decided to go back to the Giaconda. It was closed. At a loss as to where to go, Marriott spotted the steps of a music shop two doorways up.

'Here you are, mate,' he said. 'We'll do it here.'

He picked up some cardboard that was leaning against the shop's door and placed it on the steps.

'Park your bum here, my friend, and we'll start.' All the time he was laughing his head off.

So, on a cold winter's afternoon, I interviewed Steve Marriott sitting on the steps of a music shop. As we talked, occasional passers-by would recognise him. One, in fact, wanted to sell his merchandise.

'Well, come to the gig, me old son – The Packet

of Three at Dingwalls next Wednesday and we'll have a natter.'

To everyone who approached him that afternoon, he spoke with an endearing warmth and smile. Despite his status as the leader of what was basically a working pub band – the Three's set was mainly R & B, Marriott's first and true musical love, with some of the old hits, 'All Or Nothing' or 'Tin Soldier', thrown in at the end – he seemed indefatigible. He was certainly great company, keeping me amused and warm for hours with a wit, humour and candour that is rare in most musicians. It was a good interview.

At the time, I remember coming away feeling a little sorry for him. That such a major talent should now have to scrape a living playing in grotty little pubs was not my idea of fun. Ten years later, when I came to write this book, I pulled out my Marriott tape and played it again.

Listening to it I started to revise my former opinion. The quote that struck me the most was on Marriott's initial desire to play music. All he wanted, he claimed, was for The Small Faces to play the pubs and have a laugh. Stardom had denied him that and brought with it a whole lot of unwanted pressure.

He had, he said, spent his whole life 'going round the houses', only to find himself doing what he wanted to do in the first place. Now, he claimed, he was playing the pubs and having the time of his life.

I don't know if he was being one hundred per cent truthful. After all, this is a man who produced classic records and then loved to moan that he wasn't being taken seriously. And he certainly wasn't earning the kind of money that once passed through his hands.

But I did know, after a memorable afternoon with him, that there was an indestructable part of him that was still able to laugh at himself and the world, a part that kept at bay the self-destructive bitterness and cynicism that afflicts so many who have made it to the top and then seen everything fall away.

I'm really glad now that I bought him a drink.

Eyes to the left, Steve. Easy tiger!

You started off as a child actor, didn't you?

Well, that's what my mum and dad wanted me to be, I suppose. What happened was that I got this part in Oliver! – but really any kid off the street in the East End could've got the part. It weren't hard. I used to go around begging at the bus queues with a ukelele and all that, so they thought I was a born entertainer. Me mum sent me up for this audition and I shit meself. At that age I had no idea.

How old were you?

Thirteen! The reason the acting thing continued was that my school burnt down, which I got the blame for. It's a kid's dream really, innit? It all happened to Steve! What happened was that I used to have a fag upstairs in the art room and there was all this leaky gas stuff. Y'see you used to put your dog-end down a knot hole, and this time it caught the gas main and the whole fuckin' lot went up. So then there was no school to go to, and I ended up going to a drama school and paying my way through it. Y'see you get a lot of rich kids at drama schools, because their mums or dads pack 'em off there because they can't get into Eton or Harrow. Whereas I had to actually work my way through it. I used to beat up all the little rich kids for their sweets. Give me your sweets. What I'm trying to say is that I was forced into it.

Wasn't your first single for Decca a Buddy Holly song?

Yeah, I used to have the glasses with no fuckin' glass in 'em – everything. Y'know, Buddy Marriott. I loved the guy. I still do. I think he's one of the most unique-original sounds I've ever heard in my life. I still think that. Every time I put him on now I think he still fits.

When did you first become interested in music?

Ummm. Well, I started playing ukelele when I was about eight. I used to go around the old folks' homes with me mum and dad and me Auntie Joan and do things for the pensioners. And that I suppose really sums up my life (laughs).

How did you meet up with Ronnie Lane?

The first time I met Ronnie we played on the same local bill and he was with a band called The Outcasts. He was playing guitar and singing and he was great. He came into the music shop I was working in and wanted a new bass. I sold him a Harmony, cos I thought they had the best sound and also looked good at the time. That was it. He came back to my house, I cabbaged him with blues records, and a new hobby had just begun.

Was all the music you liked at the time just blues?

Yeah, rhythm and blues. It still is. I'm sorry, I'm really old-fashioned, I've never changed what I like. I can understand fads, but it's nothing a good stake through the heart wouldn't cure. I lost myself in that era and I can't get out of it. At the same time I think it's served me well because it keeps coming around. Y'know, rhythm and blues, how can you beat it?

In full flight on *Ready Steady Go*.

What sort of people did you like? Ray Charles?

In those days, Ray Charles was doing all that country and western stuff, so after 'What'd I Say' and 'Nighttime Is The Right Time' he went down in my estimation during that period and I got into people like Bobby Bland and Little Milton – people like that, who were carrying on the blues tradition as opposed to selling out to country and western.

Were you actually Mods?

To be honest with you, we were just part of something or, at least, I thought I was. These days, they say we were leaders of it – but I don't believe that. We were part of it. It was just a case of all me mates were Mods and I was a Mod. It was as simple as that. For them to say in this day and age that we're the leaders of the Mod movement, but we weren't. We were just part of the movement. We weren't no spearhead.

What sort of lifestyle did you have then?

Took pills. Stayed up all night. The Scene club until midnight. Then the Flamingo for the all-nighter. Being sick in alleyways, and ruining the jacket you just paid a fuckin' arm and a leg for.

Did you struggle to get your clothes, because they must have cost you a fortune?

Yeah, of course, but that was the main thing then. Clothes to us were essential; y'know what I mean. I don't know why because it's hard to put it into words. I've lost that verve for that whole sort of look. I just wanna be comfortable, so it's hard for me to rationalise it now.

151

It was estimated that the band spent £12,000 in one year on fab gears.

How did you feel about the other groups, because The Who were real bandwagon jumpers, weren't they?

I don't know. I wouldn't like to accuse 'em of that. I think they had a lot of money behind them and a very shrewd management. We had neither (laughs). I don't think you can call them bandwagon jumpers because they were probably as innocent to the whole fuckin' thing as we were. Now, it's become the snobbish thing to say, that The Who were manufactured. Nah, I don't think they were. They were a natural.

What did you think of the group at the time?

I thought they were marvellous. I thought we were marvellous. I thought being sick and taking pills was marvellous. I didn't analyse it. I just went for it.

How old were you when The Small Faces first started?

Sixteen. You gotta realise that when we formed The Small Faces, it was out of error. It wasn't a planned thing at all. It was a case of me getting Ronnie and Kenney slung out of their group by smashing a piano up in a pub one night. It was as simple as that. I went fuckin' beserk. Me and Ronnie got pissed and the whole gig was a mess. I think I got Ronnie the sack more times than I can remember, and so we then said – let's form a group ourselves. We had Kenney on drums and Ronnie said he'd be a bass player now, but I didn't know what I was gonna do. So I thought maybe I'd play a bit of harmonica, but we couldn't get anyone to join the group. It was the name that put 'em off. I remember sitting in this café right next door and trying to tout for guitarists. They'd say, 'Well what's

the name of the group?' – cos in those days it was a very heavy thing. I'd say (mumble) 'Small Faces,' and they'd go 'What?' 'Small Faces.' And they'd go 'Fuck off, you gotta be joking!'

What, just because of the name?

Oh yeah. It embarrassed them or something. It was against the grain. So in the end I just thought, Fuck it, I'll play guitar.

Could you play guitar then?

Not really, mate. I mean I knew E, A, D. I knew my way around it, but I wasn't proficient by any means.

What happened with Jimmy Winston?

Well, he had a slightly different mentality to us. It was a case of us and him. He was older. He was into the turned up collar with the shades on, and we couldn't really get into that. He wasn't a Mod, bless his heart, as much as he might try to be.

What sort of mentality are you talking about?

He was older. He had his own place and he was a bit of a villain on the quiet. We were more innocent because we didn't know what the Christ we were gonna do. Ours was a happy-go-lucky attitude. We formed to play weddings, cos we'd all been in better bands – no doubt about it, like musicianship wise – because we were all the youngest in our bands and we were always treated like the babies. So for us to get together, it was like, Fuck it, let's not be serious no more. Fuck trying to make it and then within three months we had a hit record – frightening!

What was it like being that young and having that kind of success?

It was scary, mate. Our nuts went and we all went a little mental.

You signed to Decca first, didn't you?

Yeah. Y'see I was dossing around this house in Loughton and Ronnie would come over occasionally. In fact we got a terrible kicking one day – the worst I've ever had and we had an audition for Don Arden the next day. Ronnie was all stitched up. I was all stitched up.

What did you get the kicking for?

Nothing. It was a bunch of Tottenham boys and apparently some Woodford or Loughton boys had gone and done up a bit of Tottenham, so the Tottenham boys all bundled out of the back of this van.

Me and Ronnie were walking home and I got one of the most severest kickings I've ever had in my life. Me, like a cunt, said 'What's it all about?' and they came back and gave me another kicking. The funny thing was the next day we were playing down the Cavern Club and Don Arden came down to check it all out. Every time Ronnie hit a note his head would bleed. My lip was out here and me eye was out here. We must have looked fearsome, but they obviously liked what they saw (laughs).

What sort of songs were you doing then?

We had about four songs. I think our repertoire got longer as we went on, cos we had this regular gig down Leicester Square Cavern – every Saturday. We gradually built a following up there. I dunno why – I think cos we used to do numbers like 'Pass The Spliff' and we wondered why the audience started to crack up laughing. But we got a good following out of four songs.

What was the first single you did for Decca?

The first single was 'What'cha Gonna Do About It' at Pye Studios with Ian Samwell.

How long was your contract with Decca for?

I've no idea. Listen, in those days I never even saw a contract.

You got ripped off a lot as well, didn't you?

Look, you go into it with your eyes open and as far as I was concerned it was better than living on brown sauce rolls. At least we had twenty quid a week guaranteed. In those days, it was great, it even meant you could hold your head up with your mum and dad. Mind you, when we got our fourth or fifth number one and we were still getting twenty quid a week . . .

At the time, though, were you actually aware of what you were creating?

No, not at all. None of us did. We didn't know if it was a cult thing or a mass thing. We had no idea. It scared us shitless, because we didn't form with any of this in mind. We were definitely unprepared for it and we tried to deal with it as best we could.

In those early records there's a real soul influence.

Well, I hope so. I don't think I've changed any. That's still what I love, and it's still where I'm at.

So you were into the whole Stax and Motown lot?

Of course. It goes without saying. In fact groups like ourselves were probably instrumental in bringing these sounds to the foreground. Taking them out of a cult thing and turning it into a mass thing. Like we'd do a cover of something and say, 'Fuck that, listen to the original.' Like 'Shake' and stuff like that.

What about bands like The Beatles?

Marvellous, I thought they were fuckin' tremendous. It was almost like the Lovin' Spoonful or something. Ronnie related to it a lot more than me, cos Ronnie could see the melodic value and artistry and all that. I weren't really looking for that. I was looking for the heart of it.

Was that the most important thing for you at that time?

Yeah. It still is (laughs). I didn't think it had that much heart. I thought it was very clever, and I was respectful of the talent, but it didn't do a lot for me, I'll be honest with ya. In fact I started taking the piss out of it – that's where 'Lazy Sunday' comes in and 'Itchycoo Park', cos it's kinda taking the piss out of the intellectuals. It got like that, y'know intellectual, so fuck all this, where's all the fun gone, y'know?

How did you take to being a teen idol?

It was fuckin' terrible. For example, when I got married, I got fuckin' sacks full of broken records and hate letters from little girls. What you have to realise, it's got absolutely nothing to do with your music; that's the heartbreaking thing. If you're at all serious about it, and I think my track record must mean I'm serious, it breaks your heart, because it means it don't matter what I play, they're not listening – not the little girls anyway. You see our audience as The Small Faces was always men. It was guys and when the chicks took over, we went down the tubes.

Whenever I look at photos of the group, you always looked close knit. Were you?

Yeah, we were. We had to be. We were up each other's arses for weeks at a time (laughs).

Well, you don't have to be. I mean, some groups hate each other and carry on for years.

Yeah, but y'see you've got to be a little dishonest to do that, and more than a little tactful, and I'm not dishonest and I'm certainly not tactful, so that didn't wash with us.

Did you have many fights within the group?

Absolutely. Me and Ronnie mainly. And over anything. My lead has fallen out. I've dropped my plectrum. It was the pressure of being screamed at and being teen idols, because the fun had gone out of it. We couldn't laugh at it any more – it was laughing at us.

When do you think the fun went out of it?

As soon as the first big cheque came in, I think, because we then had to start hiring accountants. That's when the fun goes out of it. What I'm doing now with The Packet of Three is that at the end of a show we get in the dressing room and it's a straight divvy out. Maybe it's a couple of hundred each or maybe a tenner each, but that's the fun of it. The minute you lose sight of that and you're working for someone else and big money comes in, you have to hire lawyers and accountants. There ain't no fun in that.

There seemed to be a lot of competition in those days with different groups.

Well, it was competitive. You had to try and keep topping each other. I remember Townshend sitting around our house once and, of all records 'Sha La La La Lee', to which I fuckin' hate to this day . . . Anyway, he's sittin' round there and he's all mopey, saying, 'Fucking hell, we haven't had a number one yet.' At the same time it had to be that record that done that. So it was that competitive – in his mind at least.

What do you think is the best Small Faces record that you wrote?

I think 'All Or Nothing' that I wrote takes a lot of beating. To me, if there's a song that typifies that era, then that might be it. Words regardless, cos it's only a silly love song, but the actual feel and arrangement of the thing . . . and maybe 'Tin Soldier'.

How important were words to you?

Not a lot at all. I tried to write funny words. A lot of the time they were love songs, but you didn't know why you were writing them. You were writing them cos maybe they weren't indicative of what was happening to you. The funny thing was, it happened to me three years later. So I thought, fuckin' hell, maybe I'm a prophet.

Did you write most of the words?

It's hard to say. Some did some, some did the other. Most of it was a crossover. I found towards the end, the bulk of it would be down to me because Ronnie, I think, lost interest.

How come he lost interest?

We all lost interest. I was writing songs, and I'm sure Ronnie will bear me out, I was trying to give the songs away. Ronnie and Mac would say, 'We need them.' But I'd say, 'You don't need crap. This ain't no good. It's sub-standard stuff.'

Didn't you write 'Tin Soldier' for your wife?

Yeah. Y'see that was one song that was true to life. I couldn't pull her any way I tried – money, cars, nothing. She was Rod's old lady up to that point so there's a funny thing. So I wrote her this song and it done the trick. I was gonna give it to P. P. Arnold, but she loved it so much I thought I'd hold on to it meself.

How did your stuff with P. P. Arnold come about? Was that because she was on Immediate as well?

Yeah. Y'see Immediate was like a family. We all helped each other. Mick was there, Keith was there, Chris Farlowe, Andrew Oldham. It was a lovely turnout, really it was.

A Marriott/Lane song and message for P. P. Arnold.

What about the story of Don Arden getting your parents together and telling them that all your missing money was going on your heroin habit?

Very true. I think it's disgraceful and I credited him with more class. All he had to say was, yeah, we are working them a bit hard, like seven nights a week and doubles. But he said, nah, they're on the needle. Stupid cunt. We were only smoking a bit of hash. Ain't no harm in that as it has been proved over all these years. So that sort of put our parents off the track and flung 'em up in arms against us. Nice one, Don! I'll tell you something though, without Don Arden there wouldn't be a Small Faces, so we have to say that. I think he managed us very well, money regardless. Fuck money – money only gets in the way, but what he did was that he put us over very well and opened a lot of doors. It's all very well to scream rip off and be bitter and belligerent – ain't no good to ya. Without those people you'd never get anywhere.

You had a lot of trouble with Decca, didn't you?

Well, they're all pipe-smoking cunts, ain't they? That's fucked me for Decca (laughs). It was no good for people who knew what they wanted to do and at the time we did have an idea what we wanted to do. We wanted to polish up our recording technique. We had a lot of ideas, but no time to do 'em, and in a way that's what Immediate gave us.

So Immediate gave you more recording freedom?

Yeah. In a way, though, that fucked us up as well, cos y'see in retrospect we grabbed the bull by the horns and were in the studio for a year at a time. It took a year to do Ogdens', doing the odd gig here and there, but by the time you come out and try and produce the album, you play like shit live.

What was it like when you were playing live before, with all the noise and that?

You couldn't hear it. We used to go on and not plug in. It didn't matter.

Didn't that make you really cynical, if you were writing good pop songs?

Nah, not really. In those days, you gotta remember that success was judged on the louder they screamed – and it was called excitement. The Stones got screamed at. The Who got screamed at – everyone got screamed at. The louder they screamed the more popular you were, and unfortunately that's how you were gauged. The more you can't hear the music the more popular you were – now work that out (laughs).

Didn't you at one time all live in one house together in Pimlico?

Yeah, that was great.

But wasn't that weird? I mean, you're gigging together, recording together and then you go home together. Do you think you were too close knit?

And you wonder why we hated each other! No, I think it was a great way to grow up, but that's what happened, you grew up. It was like kindergarten. Here, try this new drug. It was good fun and we had a great laugh out of it. Actually, I think we were on better terms then, than when we all got our independent pressures. Once that rot sets in, when you get an old lady and all of a sudden you pay the mortgage and the more you pay out initially, the more you gotta keep paying and it just makes both music and vibes suffer.

How did it affect you when the Mod thing started dying out?

I didn't notice it, cos I'd probably died out before it. It didn't affect me at all. I probably had eyes on America, as I stopped being a Mod before Mods stopped being Mods.

Around 1966, 1967 the hippy thing came in, I mean your response was 'Itchycoo Park'.

Yeah, taking the piss out of it. You've got to take the piss out of

yourself and other people, you must do it – you must keep the humour in the music. You can't be too fuckin' serious, because it's not that serious.

What about Ogdens'?

Well, that's not serious at all, is it? (Laughs)

Yeah, but it took a year to record it . . .

That was the only serious thing about it. I think we all got serious, and that's a problem, and then you started believing in your own publicity and stuff like that. It does happen and it can happen to the best of you. That's life.

Songs like 'Wham Bam Thank You Mam' . . .?

That was serious, y'see. Ronnie said to me when I'd written that – cos I'd written that and 'Autumn Stone' and they were our last things for Immediate as I remember. I played Ronnie 'Wham Bam Thank You Mam', and he said, 'Cor, it's a bit heavy innit?', and I said, 'Course it's fuckin' heavy', y'know, giving me the needle; but we still recorded it and in a way it was getting into Humble Pie – going in that direction.

Why did you leave the soul thing behind?

No. I didn't realise that I did. In Humble Pie I got the three black chicks and the horns back and all that, but it was too late by then. See, the only way I can do it again is by starting all over again, and that's what I'm doing with The Packet of Three. We're out there gigging every fuckin' night and it's great, sweating in the clubs again.

With the other white rock groups at the time, 1967–1968, with the Jefferson Airplane and so on, it seems to have been reflected in The Small Faces. You seemed to have gone from the really good pop stuff to the really heavy sound.

Nah, I had absolutely nothing to do with the fuckin' Chocolate Vanilla Underground and all that. I hated it. Didn't do nothing for me, mate. I think it might have done more for Ronnie than for me, cos he liked some of it. I didn't.

When you put 'The Universal' out . . .

Well, that's a right piss-take. I think that's one of the funniest songs I've ever written. At the time it went like a fuckin' bucket – down. People didn't understand it at all. Maybe it has a certain laughter value.

Didn't you write it in your back garden?

Yeah, I wrote and recorded it in my back garden. You can hear the fuckin' dogs barking – birds singing. You can hear the roadies arriving to take us to the gig. I tried to better it in the studio and couldn't do it, so I had to use the fuckin' cassette I used in the garden. Makes sense, don't it?

Why didn't you play Ogdens' live?

We could have done, if we'd had the bollocks. If we'd had the balls to

Laughter made the world go round.

take out a string and horn section – we could've done. In those days it would have been such a move to do it because no one else was doing it. Actually, it would have been perfect if we'd had the balls to do it, but I guess we didn't. I don't remember the reasons why not.

There must've been another reason for the group splitting up?

You grow apart, for Chrissakes. You're talking about people living together from the ages of seventeen to twenty-two and that's a growing up part of your life and we got to hate each other, no doubt about it. We didn't speak to each other for fuckin' years. Maybe ten years.

How did you feel about The Faces? Because Rod Stewart nicked a lot off you, didn't he?

Nah. I wouldn't like to have been him at the time and I thought he handled it beautifully – so fair enough.

That whole working class Jack the Lad thing . . . ?

Oh, that's not Rod at all. But that came to light later. He had this thing about putting me down in the press all the time. That was a bit daft cos I'd done nothing to him – but maybe it was the pressure of filling a spot.

How come you had your eyes on America?

Well, I wanted to go there. Of course, the music – I thought that would've gone without saying. It was also a new environment, because we'd been to Germany more times than we'd had hot dinners, all over Scandinavia – five, nine, ten times. The whole

point what that it was a new challenge, like Humble Pie was a new challenge.

Did The Small Faces ever do anything in America?

Never, although 'Itchycoo Park' was a hit, and 'Tin Soldier'. The funny thing is, that in America it's all Humble Pie, they've never heard of The Small Faces – except if they do their homework – and back here it's the other way round. It's more Small Faces and who's Humble Pie? But between the two I've got it captured! (Laughs)

Humble Pie were a rock group in the straight sense of the word, weren't they?

Yeah, but it was different for me. At that time, it was new anyway. There weren't many people playing that way when we first started. There's a million now, but at the time I thought it was something different to do again. Another challenge if you like, and when that got a bit tired, I introduced the horns and the black chicks. Then the rest of the group didn't want that so I left again.

What did you do after, because haven't you been living in America?

Yeah, seven years. I ended up in Atlanta for the last three years, down south, and it was great because there's a lot of good music there.

What were you doing? Recording, writing?

Yeah, I did a lot for Capricorn, which is that Macon-based label. Basically, I just worked there all the time, but it never gets over here.

What sort of stuff were you writing? Was it in the same Humble Pie sort of vein?

I dunno. I can't be the judge of that. I don't write in any vein.

What did you think of punk?

Great. Exciting. Every now and again, you need that fuckin' kick up the arse, and that was great. Unfortunately, the musicianship was a bit fucked, but then so was I when I started, so I could identify with that totally, and good luck to 'em.

How did it feel playing with a group like Humble Pie after The Small Faces?

Different. I can tell ya, if you listen to the early Humble Pie albums, like Town And Country, it's very similar to The Small Faces. When we went to America, we were playing acoustic guitars on stage, but the Americans wouldn't buy it. They didn't want it and our manager was saying (American accent), 'No, stick to the rock, stick to the rock.' So we went with that, and it just got fuckin' boring (laughs). Then I got the three black chicks and the horn section. I thought it was great at the time.

How long did Humble Pie last?

From about 1969 to 1974. Five years.

You then did a Small Faces reunion with an LP. Why?

Why not? What happened was this. We did a fuckin' video for 'Itchycoo Park' – which was a hit again, right. They'd released it – and it goes in the top ten. I got a phone call from Kenney Jones – Would you do a video for it? So I said, sure. We all got together, did the video and screamed at each other, cos you got to remember we hadn't seen each other. Screamed at each other and fell in love with each other again. That's why. Regardless of the merit of the album, it was done in all good faith, so at least it introduced four people back together.

You also did a gig at the Rainbow, how did that go?

Shocking (laughs).

What about the LP? What was that like?

I liked it. It was very different. It wasn't what was expected of us, which I always like. I like to do that. Unfortunately, it goes up your own arse a lot of the time, but I still like to do that. I don't like following fuckin' trends or doing what you're supposed to do. I hate that.

So, after that you were working for Capricorn. Did you make much money out of it?

No, of course not. Look, what I've had I've fuckin' thrown up in the air, and what's come down I've spent. I've had a great fuckin' life. If I weren't me I'd be envious. Mind you, I wouldn't let me into my dressing room either. I've had everything I wanted out of life. All I'm doing now by gigging all the time is pleasing myself. Which is how it started. That's why The Small Faces were formed.

So you've come full circle.

Yeah, and I love it.

What sort of things did you want out of life?

Happiness is hard to buy. I dunno, just to be happy really, just to be able to laugh at it all.

What sort of things make you happy?

Brown sauce rolls. The same things I started off with really. You realise, by going round the houses, that your original idea was dead right. You don't need all this fuckin' money. It's bullshit, but until you have it, how do you know that? We've got a drummer in the band now, who wants to be a star so bad. He's brilliant, mind you. I hope he is a star – so that he can look at it and go, 'Cor, fuckin' hell, I don't want this' (laughs). You 'ave to do that first I suppose.

What made you come back to England and start the group up again?

Mmm, I was going through a divorce and stuff and I missed my family. I hadn't seen 'em for seven years. I'd seen 'em once in that seven years for about two weeks. I heard my father was ill, which worried me. So I came home and fell in love with it again.

What, England?

Yeah. I think the tax situation had died down, y'know what I mean, in as much as I could live here again. At least I haven't had my collar felt yet, but I might do (laughs).

When did you start this new group up? Last year?

Yeah, I did it for a laugh. This is always what happens though. You do something for a laugh – and you can't lose.

What do you think about your audiences now, because I hear you get a lot of Mods down there?

Yeah, it's funny. You get the fuckin' tattooed long-haired Humble Pie freaks, with Steve tattooed across their chests – bless their hearts. You get all these Mods, and bless their hearts. Then you get, like, punks that have come because their big brother said – great. It's a right interesting cross-section. It seems to work. Like I said, we didn't start it for nothing but a laugh, and all of a sudden it's like interviews and records out. Let me tell you, this is how it started with The Small Faces. It's almost like déjà vu, cos I did it for a giggle. We started playing weddings locally – Sawbridge Workman's Memorial Hall Presents Steve Marriott – right. It was a joke. Just to have a play, a giggle. It's doing it again. All of a sudden, I've got a fuckin' album coming out. I've done nothing. I just played live, someone taped it and I've mixed it, and it's come right. I'm sitting here doing an interview with you, and it's all déjà vu.

I was wondering how you felt about The Small Faces connection and Weller and him being really into you.

I think it's marvellous. I don't know what I've done to deserve it. I really don't. I just think I'm a lucky boy.

Do you ever look back on it, with The Small Faces, and see how good they actually were?

I can see what other people saw in it, but then again it's very difficult to look from the inside and see how good you were, because you knew all your faults, so you knew how bad you were in actual fact.

What sort of faults?

Faults? Well, faults – how you get around doing this and that, you used this because you couldn't fucking do that – but that's for me to think and not for you to know (laughs).

Do you still do drugs?

Nah, I don't. Mind you, I've tried everything and nothing grabbed me hard enough that I wanted to carry on doing it. I think coke was about the nearest I got to ever having to have some.

157

Has it ever really fucked you up, drugs?

It must've done, somewhere along the line (laughs). I can't point my finger on it. I won't buy the stuff no more. Unfortunately, it's a lovely fantasy world to live in, but you don't half need a lot of money to live there.

What about today's groups?

I think Big Country sound like Bonanza (hums tune). As I say, most of the groups today, it's nothing a good stake through the heart wouldn't cure, y'know? Aztec Camera I think are quite interesting, funny enough. I love Paul Young's voice. I don't like the choice of material, cos he could do so much with a good voice like that. He's got a raw voice which has been put in a smooth background. Now don't laugh at that voice, mate. He has got a great voice.

Yeah maybe, I dunno.

I know. Fuck off, I'm a singer, I'm telling ya. It's like you can say he's a great writer, and I go I don't know. I love the singers in UB40, like the two white kids that sing. Fuckin' hell, they're frightening. Things like that.

What about Weller, did you like him?

Look, I'll be honest with ya. I've only seen The Jam once on a video, and I thought it reminded me of me in the old days. So for me to say that – sure I like me (laughs). It's not like I can really judge 'em. They looked exactly like we did and played similarly. At the same time, I admire their taste (laughs).

This is a question from Weller. Why don't you get back to your soul roots and do a blistering soul/funk record?

Why don't you come to a gig, ya cunt? Why don't you buy my next album and 'ave a listen. Funny thing is, he [Paul Weller] probably don't know what I've done in years, cos it's all been over there.

What about your favourite singers?

Same as ever. Little Richard. Bobby Bland. James Brown. Inez Foxx. Inez has to be one of the best. Mavis Staples. I rung Stax from England once – about 1972 – and said, 'Can I produce Inez?' They said, 'Who's this?' I said, 'Steve Marriott.' They hung up.

Would you like to get into producing?

I think that's the only way to go. It takes a lot out of my body these days. I've broken so many bones in the course of the fun, that it takes a hell of a lot out of me now. I think I'll give it my best shot for a couple of years, have a right go, which I'm doing. I'm playing the clubs, sweating and enjoying myself. I'll do that and then I'll have to get into producing. I should pass on any knowledge, if there's any knowledge that I've learned. You shouldn't keep it a secret.

What's your fave record of all time? Off the top of your head.

(Pause) 'Green Onions' (laughs).

Stephen Peter Marriott.

158

SINGLES

1. 'What'cha Gonna Do About It'
b/w 'What's A Matter Baby'.
Released: 6 August 1965 (DECCA F 12208)
Chart position: Number 14.

2. 'I've Got Mine' b/w 'It's Too Late'.
Released: 5 November 1965 (DECCA F 12276)
Chart position: Failed to chart.

3. 'Sha La La La Lee' b/w 'Grow Your Own'.
Released: 28 January 1966 (DECCA F 12317)
Chart position: Number 3.

4. 'Hey Girl' b/w 'Almost Grown'.
Released: 6 May 1966 (DECCA F 12393)
Chart position: Number 10.

5. 'All Or Nothing' b/w 'Understanding'.
Released: 5 August 1966 (DECCA F 12470)
Chart position: Number 1.

6. 'My Mind's Eye' b/w 'I Can't Dance With You'.
Released: 11 November 1966 (DECCA F 12500)
Chart position: Number 4.

7. 'I Can't Make It' b/w 'Just Passing'.
Released: 3 March 1967 (Immediate recordings on DECCA F 12565)
Chart position: Number 26.

8. 'Patterns' b/w 'E Too D'.
Released: 26 May 1967 (Unauthorised release DECCA F 12619)
Chart position: Failed to chart.

9. 'Here Come The Nice' b/w 'Talk To You'.
Released: 2 June 1967 (IMMEDIATE IM 050)
Chart position: Number 12.

10. 'Itchycoo Park' b/w 'I'm Only Dreaming'.
Released: 4 August 1967 (IMMEDIATE IM 057)
Chart position: Number 3.
US chart position: Number 16.

11. 'Tin Soldier' b/w 'I Feel Much Better'.
Released: 2 December 1967 (IMMEDIATE IM 062)
Chart position: Number 9.

12. 'Lazy Sunday' b/w 'Rollin' Over'.
Released: 5 April 1968 (IMMEDIATE IM 064)
Chart position: Number 2.

1965—69

13. 'The Universal'
b/w 'Donkey Rides, A Penny, A Glass'.
Released: 28 June 1968 (IMMEDIATE IM 069)
Chart position: Number 16.

14. 'Afterglow (Of Your Love)'
b/w 'Wham Bam Thank You Mam'.
Released: 7 March 1969 (IMMEDIATE IM 077)
Chart position: Number 36.

ALBUMS

1. SMALL FACES
Side One: Shake; Come On Children; You Better Believe It; It's Too Late; One Night Stand; What'cha Gonna Do About It.
Side Two: Sorry She's Mine; Own Up Time; You Need Loving; Don't Stop What You're Doing; E Too D; Sha La La La Lee.
Released: 6 May 1966 (DECCA LK 4790)
Chart position: Number 3.

2. FROM THE BEGINNING
Side One: Runaway; My Mind's Eye; Yesterday Today & Tomorrow; That Man; My Way Of Giving; Hey Girl; (Tell Me) Have You Ever Seen Me.
Side Two: Come Back And Take This Hurt Off Me; All Or Nothing; Baby Don't Do It; Plum Nellie; Sha La La La Lee; You Really Got A Hold On Me; What'cha Gonna Do About It.
Released: 2 June 1967 (DECCA LK 4879)
Chart position: Number 17.

3. SMALL FACES
Side One: (Tell Me) Have You Ever Seen Me; Something I Want To Tell You; Feeling Lonely; Happy Boys Happy; Things (Are Going To Get

Better); My Way Of Giving; Green Circles.
Side Two: Become Like You; Get Yourself Together; All Our Yesterdays; Talk To You; Show Me The Way; Up The Wooden Hills To Bedfordshire; Eddie's Dreaming.
Released: 23 June 1967 (IMMEDIATE IMLP 008)
Chart position: Number 12.

4. OGDENS' NUT GONE FLAKE
Side One: Ogdens' Nut Gone Flake; Afterglow (Of Your Love); Long Ago's And World's Apart; Rene; Song Of A Baker; Lazy Sunday.
Side Two: Happiness Stan; Rollin' Over; The Hungry Intruder; The Journey; Mad John; Happy Days Toy Town.
Released: 24 May 1968 (IMMEDIATE IMLP 012)
Chart position: Number 1.

5. THE AUTUMN STONE
Record One (Studio Recordings): The Autumn Stone; Collibosher; Red Balloon; Call It Something Nice; Sha La La La Lee; All Or Nothing; The Universal; I Can't Make It; Here Come The Nice; Lazy Sunday; Afterglow (Of Your Love).

Record Two (Live Recordings): Rollin' Over; If I Were A Carpenter; Every Little Bit Hurts; My Mind's Eye; Tin Soldier; Just Passing; Itchycoo Park; Hey Girl; Wide Eyed Girl On The Wall; What'cha Gonna Do About It; Wham Bam Thank You Mam.
Released: November 1969 (IMMEDIATE IMAL 012)
Chart position: Failed to chart.

BIBLIOGRAPHY

Rod Stewart and the Changing Faces, John Pidgeon (Panther)
Mods, Richard Barnes (Eel Pie)
Quant by Quant, Mary Quant (Pan)
Before I Get Old, Dave Marsh (Plexus)
All Our Yesterdays, Terry Rawlings (Riot Stories)
Life – The '60's (Time Inc. Publishing)
Classic Albums, compiled by John Pidgeon for Radio One (BBC)
'Happy Boys Happy' by Roland Schmitt & Uli Twelker (1993, Germany)

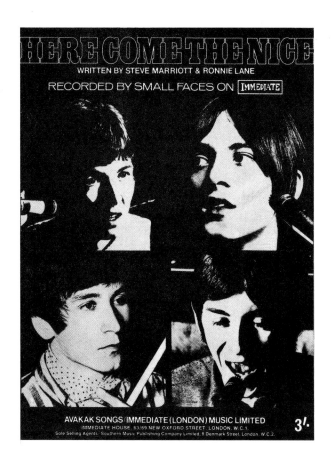